ORGANIZING
THE 1%

ORGANIZING
THE 1%

HOW CORPORATE POWER WORKS

WILLIAM K. CARROLL
& J.P. SAPINSKI

FERNWOOD PUBLISHING
HALIFAX & WINNIPEG

Editing: Curran Faris
Cover design: John van der Woude
Printed and bound in Canada

Published by Fernwood Publishing
32 Oceanvista Lane, Black Point, Nova Scotia, B0J 1B0
and 748 Broadway Avenue, Winnipeg, Manitoba, R3G 0X3
www.fernwoodpublishing.ca

Fernwood Publishing Company Limited gratefully acknowledges the
financial support of the Government of Canada, the Manitoba Department
of Culture, Heritage and Tourism under the Manitoba Publishers Marketing
Assistance Program and the Province of Manitoba, through the Book
Publishing Tax Credit, for our publishing program. We are pleased to work
in partnership with the Province of Nova Scotia to develop and promote
our creative industries for the benefit of all Nova Scotians. We acknowledge
the support of the Canada Council for the Arts, which last year invested
$153 million to bring the arts to Canadians throughout the country.

Canada   Canada Council   Conseil des arts   NOVA SCOTIA   Manitoba
for the Arts   du Canada

Library and Archives Canada Cataloguing in Publication

Carroll, William K., author
Organizing the 1% : how corporate power works / William
K. Carroll, J.P. Sapinski.

Includes bibliographical references and index.
Issued in print and electronic formats.
ISBN 978-1-55266-890-0 (softcover).--ISBN 978-1-77363-081-6
(EPUB).--ISBN 978-1-77363-082-3 (Kindle)

1. Corporate power--Canada. 2. Capitalism--Canada.
I. Sapinski, J. P., 1976-, author II. Title.

HD2809 C37765 2018   306.3'420971   C2018-903707-5
                    C2018-903979-5

MIX
Paper from
responsible sources
FSC
www.fsc.org   FSC® C013916

CONTENTS

ACKNOWLEDGEMENTS

In writing this book we have been supported by The Corporate Mapping Project, a university-community partnership funded by the Social Sciences and Humanities Research Council of Canada, hosted by the University of Victoria and co-directed by William K. Carroll and Shannon Daub <www.corporatemapping.ca>. We have learned a great deal from colleagues on the Project and from studies completed under its umbrella, and have tried to incorporate many of those insights into the text. Wayne Antony took an early interest in this book, and his encouragement and critical feedback (as well as comments from an anonymous reviewer) have been crucial to its completion. We also appreciate the attention to detail on the production side that Beverley Rach, Curran Faris and Jason Miller have provided. Any inadequacies that remain in the work are our responsibility. Any inadequacies that remain in the work are our responsibility.

William K. Carroll and J.P. Sapinski
May 2018

Chapter 1

WHAT ON EARTH IS CORPORATE POWER?

Corporations and Capitalism

Take a stroll in Toronto's central business district and you will encounter seven of Canada's ten tallest buildings, each one an icon of glinting glass and steel, protected by elaborate security systems. If you look down rather than up, you may notice the occasional homeless person, bundled into a sleeping bag, or begging for spare change. The juxtaposition of extreme poverty in the midst of unparalleled wealth can be arresting. What is it that creates such a paradox and such injustice? The skyscrapers are home to Canada's largest corporations and financial institutions; in fact, five of the tallest are headquarters to Canada's five biggest banks.[1] Each building was created by construction workers, using materials produced by other workers. Yet those workers (actually, all workers) have nothing to do with the business strategies hatched in the executive suites within, nor for that matter do the homeless. If you venture a kilometre northeast from the skyscrapers, you'll arrive at Toronto's most impoverished neighbourhood, Moss Park. You'll see lots of dilapidated housing projects, food banks and soup kitchens, and even more homeless people. The disconnect between corporate opulence — the elite 1% of the wealthy 1% — and abject destitution will be, at that point, complete. Statistics sum it up: at least 35,000 people sleep without a home every night in Canada, and in Toronto alone nearly 100 people died homeless in 2017. Meanwhile, Canada's 100 highest paid CEOs earned more than $10 million each in 2016, which is 209 times the average income for Canadians and 316 times more than someone earning $15 an hour.[2]

In our everyday worlds, we actually encounter corporate power at every turn, though we may not notice. The goods and services we consume, the jobs we hold or aspire to hold and the mass and social media that enliven (or perhaps deaden) our lives are all organized primarily on a corporate basis; the same is true for the pensions that, if we are fortunate, await us at the close of our careers. Corporate power is in the background, and often in the foreground, of news narratives, and of course news itself (along with popular culture and entertainment) is produced as a source of profit for media corporations. Corporate power is so pervasive that, like fish swimming in the water, we may be altogether unaware of its presence. In this book, we provide an overview of how corporate power operates in Canada today: how it organizes the 1% economically, politically and culturally. But we also lay out a basic history of how we got to where we are, and we consider what alternatives may be in the offing for the future.

We write as critics of corporate power, its social inequities, its ecological maladies and the sharp limits it places upon a democratic way of life. By exercising political power in a way not available to ordinary citizens, large corporations and those controlling them are able to appropriate the larger part of the wealth created in the country, which exacerbate social inequality. Similarly, corporations rely on lenient environmental regulations to maintain and increase profits by transferring ecological costs to governments and citizens. Sometimes social critics are dismissed as "biased" or dreamers. Our approach, however, is evidence based and realistic.

First, we provide a framework for understanding corporate power within contemporary capitalism. We then dig into the history of corporate capitalism in Canada, and, in later chapters, map out the "modalities" of corporate power: the forms that it takes in the economic, cultural and political fields. To fix a troublesome problem, we need to understand it in its fullness. Corporate power is such a problem, for people and for the natural world in which we are immersed. Unlike fish in water, people can change their world. Corporate power is actually a recent development in human history, and because it was created by humans, it can be undone and transcended. Our hope is that what follows will help you situate your life within the structure of corporate power in Canada, in a way that gets beyond one of corporate power's most persuasive, and misleading, pretenses: that there is no alternative to contemporary capitalism.

So, what is this thing called corporate power? Put simply, it is the power that accrues to enormous concentrations of capital, which, in contemporary societies, are organized as large corporations (see Box 1.1). To understand corporate power, we need to unpack what capital is and how control of capital means control of the human, technological, financial and natural resources through which human needs are satisfied. Control of capital places corporate owners, directors and top executives in a dominant position in economic decision-making, including over the

---

BOX 1.1. CAPITAL

Capital is usually understood as a stock of something that we can draw on in various situations, such as a sum of money that can be used to cover expenses or invested to obtain a return. Sociologists often talk, metaphorically, about "social capital" to describe the network of relationships individuals can draw on when they need support.

The way we use capital in this book draws from the Marxist tradition and departs from the common meaning of the word. For Marx, "capital is not a thing, but a social relation between persons, established by the instrumentality of things." The money we may have in our bank account is in reality a representation of the amount of goods and services — the products of labour performed elsewhere — we can purchase from businesses. This money (along with the business that employs the workers and sells the product) mediates between purchaser and producers, whether the latter be autoworkers in Windsor, garment workers in Dhaka or peasants in rural Mexico. In this sense, capital is the great mediator, as economist Michael Lebowitz has observed.

Beyond simply money though, Marx views capital as a self-expanding process, of which money is but one moment. The process begins when a capitalist invests money capital to purchase means of production (machinery, raw materials, etc.) and to hire workers. Money capital is thereby converted into productive capital, as workers are set to work, producing new commodities. As those goods and services find buyers, capital once again takes the form of money. But since the labour performed by workers has added new value, the capitalist now has more money capital than was advanced initially; in other words, the capitalist has turned a profit. Part of that profit is then reinvested by the capitalist into expanded production, and the process of self-expansion begins anew.[3]

flow of resources to new initiatives, which shapes the future. Such control includes major economic decisions about what, when, where and how to produce. And this control relegates workers, communities and governments to a position of unilateral dependence. As sociologist Peter Blau pointed out more than half a century ago, such dependence obliges the rest of us to comply with the dictates and wishes of those who dominate or else lose access to jobs and revenue. From its base in the economy, corporate power reaches into other areas — political and cultural — shaping the institutions, agendas, policies, discourses and values that add up to an entire way of life. That way of life is known as corporate capitalism.[4]

CAPITALISM AS A WAY OF LIFE

By its celebrants, capitalism is praised as a free society. Freedom is secured by the "free market system." Everyone has the opportunity to earn and spend money as they choose. This freedom of choice defines our political system — known as a liberal order — and extends through elections to the choice of political leaders. In this perspective, competition is an inherently progressive force. Individuals compete with each other as they try to get ahead; businesses compete with each other as they try to maximize profit, and all that competition unleashes human talent and innovation, to the betterment of everyone. As the economy grows we all become more prosperous and fulfilled, even as the most talented and determined rise to the top and reap the lion's share of all the material benefits created. The freedom to acquire private property (not simply personal property like a house and car, but capital), and to dispose of it as one pleases, underwrites what Karl Marx, capitalism's most important critic, called "a very Eden of the innate rights of man."

> There alone rule Freedom, Equality, Property and Bentham. Freedom, because both buyer and seller of a commodity, say of labour-power, are constrained only by their own free will. They contract as free agents, and the agreement they come to, is but the form in which they give legal expression to their common will. Equality, because each enters into relation with the other, as with a simple owner of commodities, and they exchange equivalent for equivalent. Property, because each disposes only of what is his own. And Bentham, because each looks only to himself.

The only force that brings them together and puts them in relation with each other, is the selfishness, the gain and the private interests of each. Each looks to himself only, and no one troubles himself about the rest, and just because they do so, do they all, in accordance with the pre-established harmony of things, or under the auspices of an all-shrewd providence, work together to their mutual advantage, for the common weal and in the interest of all.[5]

With Marx, we can acknowledge these basic features of capitalism, which form the core of "liberal ideology": the belief system that legitimates capitalism. In any ideology there are practical truths, which make it persuasive. Yet with Marx we can also dig deeper, beneath the surface-level appearances of capitalism, to uncover sources of power and inequality.

The "free market system" that liberals celebrate does not actually float free. Before anything can be bought and sold, it must be produced. All those products placed on the "free market" — even the skyscrapers that grace Toronto's central business district — result from labour processes that are organized within relations of production. Often when we think of a marketplace, a traditional farmers' market comes to mind. In such a market, one might find ten different vendors of potatoes, who are also the farmers who grew and harvested those potatoes. Owning their own means of production (land, seeds, farm equipment) and working on their own account, such farmers are "independent commodity producers." In theory, a market society in which all participants were independent commodity producers — selling to and buying from each other — would represent the liberal ideal.

But such a society has never existed. In actual societies, independent commodity production has always existed alongside other class-based relations of production. For instance, although at the time of the American Revolution there were various independent commodity producers (and small-scale capitalists) in the northern colonies, the slave system of the southern colonies was actually dominant in what became the USA. Most leaders of that revolution — George Washington, Thomas Jefferson and others — were slaveholders. According to historian Gerald Horne, the "revolution" was in great part a counter-revolution led by the founding fathers to preserve their right to enslave others.[6]

Obviously, within contemporary capitalism, farmers' markets are the exception, not the rule. Most markets are dominated by a few big corporate players, and roughly nine-tenths of the population do not own businesses and work for wages and salaries. What underlies the market is not independent commodity production but capitalist production. To comprehend the difference, we need to understand what capital is. To quote Marx again, "capital is not a thing, but a social relation between persons, established by the instrumentality of things."[7]

Specifically, capitalism, as an economic system, is based on a *class relation of exploitation* between capitalists and wage workers (labour). In all capitalist societies, a small dominant class owns and controls the main means of production, transport/communication, commerce and finance. The nine-tenths of the population who are dependent on employment as a source of income are linked into the economy not through farmers' markets but through labour markets. They sell their "labour -power" — their capacity to work — to employers, in exchange for wages and salaries that enable them to buy what they need to live. On the other side of the relationship between capitalists and workers, capitalists buy labour-power from workers in order to reap a profit from whatever the workforce accomplishes under their direction. In the class relation that comprises capitalism, the worker's motive is to meet her needs, but the capitalist's is to grow his fortune.[8]

Most people think of exploitation as an exceptional situation in which a particular group of workers is victimized by an unscrupulous employer who cheats them out of wages, for example. But in actuality, exploitation is a systemic feature of capitalism. This is hard to see, due to the market element of capitalism, particularly the labour market. Digging beneath the market, into the realm of production, we notice that the labour-power workers exchange for a wage is set to work in producing goods and services of greater value than the capitalist's initial investments. The difference between the value of those initial investments (for land, buildings, raw materials, technology and the purchase of labour-power) and the revenue from the sale of the product provides the capitalist's profit. If this difference did not occur, if workers did not create surplus value, in excess of the costs of production, the capitalist would have no reason to hire them. As economist Jim Stanford puts it:

Productive human effort ("work," broadly defined) is clearly the only way to transform the things we harvest from our natural environment into useful goods and services. In this sense, work is the source of all value added.[9]

When we scale up from individual businesses to the system overall, this means that workers earn, on average, the going wage, and capitalists claim, on average, the going rate of profit. But the entire profit capitalists, as an entire class, claim is simply the economic surplus that the entire workforce, the working class, has produced. At the close of each working week, workers are paid the value of their labour-power (enabling them on average to live at the basic standard for employees), but their labour has created new value worth more than what they have been paid as wages. The whole of the new wealth created by workers is appropriated by capitalists. This is what systemic exploitation means. By owning and controlling the means of production, capitalists, rather than workers, or workers and capitalists together, own and control the economic surplus. Owning and controlling the economic surplus means power over workers in production but also power over shaping a future that depends upon how capitalists dispose of society's economic surplus, that is, on how they invest. This is, in fact, the fundamental basis of corporate power.

Plotting the division of Canada's Net National Income into labour income (wages and salaries) and economic surplus (corporate profits + interest and investment income), as shown in Figure 1.1, gives some concrete idea of how all this works. Here we can see roughly how much of the new wealth created each year by labour is claimed by capitalists as corporate profit, interest and investment income. The share appropriated by capitalists has increased from 22.4 percent in the 1960s to 29.0 percent in the 1970s, and it has stabilized slightly above 30 percent since then. This reflects how the automation wave of the 1970s allowed corporations to divert a larger part of social wealth to their owners, meanwhile very little of that new wealth made it to the workers whose labour produced that wealth.

Figure 1.1. The trend in Canada is for corporations to claim a larger share of net national income.[10]

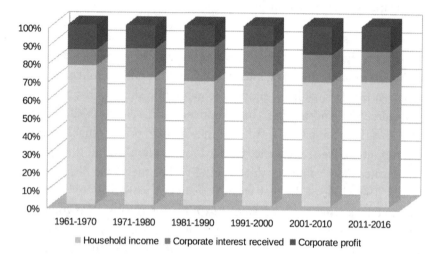

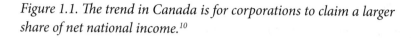

Household income ■ Corporate interest received ■ Corporate profit

The economic surplus that accrues to capitalists can also be roughly calculated at the level of individual corporations. Four decades ago, historian Leo Johnson calculated the amount of surplus per worker in eleven major Canadian corporations. He found that the employees of these corporations, comprising just 1.5 percent of all income earners, generated an economic surplus for the corporations and their controlling capitalists equivalent to the total income received by the poorest 1,400,000 earners.[11]

Workers lacking their own means of production have little choice but to be exploited by employers. This is how they earn a living. But what about capitalists? Must they exploit workers, or could they behave otherwise? Again, a systemic analysis illuminates. Capitalists control wealth through many competing firms, the largest of which are giant corporations. Within the market economy, capitalists do compete for shares of the economic surplus that their class as a whole appropriates from workers. As political economist Ben Fine observes:

> [for capitalists] a situation of competitive accumulation exists, the condition of survival being to take part. In brief, capital as self-expanding value creates competition, which is fought by accumulation. The need to accumulate is felt by each individual capitalist as an external coercive force. Accumulate or die; there are few exceptions.[12]

Capitalists compete with each other in the quest to claim a sufficient share of the economic surplus — an above-average profit — to keep them "in the game." Their class position as capitalists is at stake. The alternative is absorption into another capitalist's enterprise, or bankruptcy. Capitalist competition is waged by cutting the cost of production. They do this through lowering wages (including the outsourcing of cheap labour), externalizing costs (tax avoidance, avoiding environmental costs of pollution and resource depletion) or technical innovations. Competition also occurs across economic sectors (and regions). Capitalists are motivated to move from lower-profit to higher-profit sectors, creating rust belts here and zones of hyper-development there. Moreover, in corporate capitalism, the vast scale of production requires an elaborate apparatus for financing new production and for getting commodities to consumers. So, the economic surplus is competitively subdivided not only among industrial corporations but also among other kinds of capitalist corporations, from finance and real estate to retail commerce, as investors of whatever stripe strive for above-average rates of return.[13]

All this profit-driven competition has led historically to remarkable advances in the "forces of production" — the techniques, technologies, knowledges and other means by which humans are linked to the rest of nature. However, these advances are always contained within capitalism's exploitative relations of production. Each capitalist strives to minimize the wage bill, which means keeping wages in check and introducing innovations that improve productivity and reduce the need for labour. Yet, for the system as a whole, these business strategies limit the capacity of workers-consumers to buy the cornucopia of products their own labour has produced, generating a trend toward under-consumption. At the same time, as production becomes more capital-intensive, the actual basis of profit — labour — shrinks relative to investments in machinery and technology, and this dampens the overall rate of profit. These problems add up to what sociologist James O'Connor has called capitalism's "first contradiction" between the advancing forces of production and relations of production encapsulated in the capital-labour relation.[14]

In the short term, the financial sector can mitigate this contradiction. Credit cards and the like can temporarily extend consumer demand, and investors unhappy with the rate of return on industrial capital can shift into the paper economy (stocks, bonds, derivatives and hedge funds, etc.).

Yet these fixes are superficial. They prolong a boom economy by postpon-
ing the inevitable slump. When the financial bubble bursts, investment
contracts. Weaker firms go under, and the remaining capitalists become
risk-averse. As investment contracts, many workers lose their jobs, and
with that, consumer spending tanks. Capitalism enters a phase of crisis,
stagnation and, for many, intensified misery.

Although liberal economics argues that capitalism naturally tends
toward equilibrium between supply and demand, production and consumption, and investment and spending, the history of capitalism shows
this to be untrue. Since the late 1920s, Canada has experienced twelve
crises, as Philip Cross and Philippe Bergevin show (Table 1.1). The two
crises that comprised the Great Depression in the 1930s were most severe
(category 5), but the three post-1980 crises have been only slightly less
substantial in impact and persistence.[15]

Table 1.1. Economic crises since the First World War[16]

Monthly Peak	Monthly Trough	Category (1 to 5)
April 1929	February 1933	5
November 1937	June 1938	5
August 1947	March 1948	2
April 1951	December 1951	3
July 1953	July 1954	4
March 1957	January 1958	3
March 1960	March 1961	3
December 1974	March 1975	2
January 1980	June 1980	1
June 1981	October 1982	4
March 1990	April 1992	4
October 2008	May 2009	4

Crisis evokes strong images, from the crash of 1929 (bankrupted stock-
brokers jumping to their deaths from skyscrapers) to the crash of 2008
(homeless families evicted from houses purchased under dubious credit
arrangements). Crisis exposes the irrationality of capitalism as a way of life
and intensifies struggles from below. Examples of such struggles include

the industrial union movement of the 1930s and the Occupy movement of 2011–12. But crisis is also capitalism's means of self-preservation. For the surviving firms, the "destruction of capital" — the devaluation of paper assets and bankruptcy of the weaker firms — improves conditions for profitable accumulation, as do the falling wages that accompany wide-spread unemployment. So it is that crises are followed by upswings in accumulation, giving capitalism its well-known boom/bust business cycle.

Marx saw major accumulation crises as endemic to capitalism. They express a central contradiction in this way of life. As a result of capitalist competition, society's productive forces expand continuously. Yet the capacity to put those forces to good use within thriving human commu-nities is severely limited by the very antagonistic relation between capital and labour that is the source of profit and the basis for production:

> The growing incompatibility between the productive develop-ment of society and its hitherto existing relations of production expresses itself in bitter contradictions, crises, spasms. The violent destruction of capital not by relations external to it, but rather as a condition of its self-preservation, is the most striking form in which advice is given it to be gone and to give room to a higher state of social production. ... These contradictions, of course, lead to explosions, crises, in which momentary suspension of all labour and annihilation of a great part of the capital violently lead it back to the point where it is enabled [to go on] fully employing its productive powers without committing suicide.[17]

Crises momentarily shrink capital. According to Statistics Canada, during the last major crisis Canada's GDP contracted in the first quarter of 2009 by 2.2 percent, only to grow by 1.2 percent in the first quarter of 2010. Indeed, the clear historical trend is for capital to grow. Capitalists take some of the surplus for themselves in the form of personal incomes that dwarf workers' wages. But they also accumulate capital by reinvesting some of the profit in more extensive production. The system as a whole expands, pulling more and more human practices and natural processes into its vortex and colonizing new frontiers. Just as capitalists, if they are to remain capitalists, cannot avoid exploiting workers, the system as a whole must grow — the alternative is collapse, as the incentive to invest disappears. Yet capitalism is part of a complex ecosystem — planet Earth

— whose web of life is sustained not through endless growth but in an ever-changing balance that is threatened by capital's constant movement. There is a deep contradiction between the capitalist logic of endless growth and the Earth's finite character. The key question, posed by geographer David Harvey, is how capital can continue to accumulate and expand in perpetuity "when it seems to involve a doubling if not tripling in the size of the astonishing physical transformations that have been wrought across planet earth in the last forty years."[18]

CORPORATE CAPITALISM
IN THE WEB OF LIFE

To pose this question is to point to what James O'Connor calls capitalism's "second contradiction," which has become especially acute in our era. Competition pushes individual capitalists to externalize costs not only onto society but also onto the ecosystem. The result is a strong tendency to degrade the "conditions of production," that is, the ecological systems behind fundamental resources such as water and soil, as well as the climate itself.[19]

Indeed, legal scholar Joel Bakan has characterized the corporation as an "externalizing machine — the corporation's built-in compulsion to externalize its costs is at the root of many of the world's social and environmental ills." The point in externalization is to reduce the cost of doing business by making someone else pay. Business-friendly governments often help out, through weak regulations and low tax and royalty rates to attract investment by boosting profits. Since the 1990s in Alberta, for instance, a lax regulatory regime allowed oil and gas companies to abandon wells without proper remediation after the resource has been extracted. A recent study estimated that "17,000 out of 170,000 abandoned wells in rural Alberta are leaking methane and that leaks at 3,400 wells could pose a risk to the public." In cities like Edmonton and Calgary, more than 1,000 abandoned wells have yet to be located and tested for leakage. In B.C., after the dam retaining the tailings pond at Mount Polley mine collapsed in August 2014, sending 25 million cubic metres of contaminated effluent into Quesnel Lake, the province spent $40 million cleaning up the disaster. Investigators concluded the failure resulted from a design flaw in the dam, but the company responsible for its construction, Imperial Metals (owned by Murray Edwards, a leading donor to the B.C. Liberal Party, then in power) was never fined or charged. Indeed, the government's immediate response was to help Edwards spin a public-relations response that would protect other proposed mining projects from criticism.[20]

Pollution as a means of externalizing costs is an instance of something more general. World-systems theorist Jason Moore notes that, in concert with the exploitation of labour, capitalists have always boosted the profitability of their investments by appropriating "Cheap Nature." By incorporating the so-called free gifts of nature as an ecological surplus, capitalism has kept costs of key inputs to production low, from energy, water and raw materials to the food that provides subsistence to workers. Historically, this appropriation has often occurred through colonization and land-grabs on resource frontiers. For capitalism, nature has served as both tap and sink. From beaver pelts in early colonial Canada to light sweet crude oil in post-World War Two Alberta, business has tapped nature's bounty. At the same time, nature has been a sink, absorbing capitalism's waste, as the examples of externalization cited above show. According to sociologist Allan Schnaiberg, capitalism's endless growth puts us all on an accelerating "treadmill of production," extracting resources (many of them non-renewable) and depositing waste in greater and greater quantities.[21]

When capitalism inhabited only a small region of the planet, between the sixteenth and nineteenth centuries, these ecologically problematic tendencies had only local consequences: a ravaged forest here, a polluted river there. But with the full-fledged globalization of corporate capitalism in the late twentieth century and the closing of resource frontiers, the era of Cheap Nature and low environmental impact drew to a close. Both the costs of production and the impact of ecological degradation started rising. Climate change epitomizes what Moore calls the "unsavory convergence" of nature-as-tap and nature-as-sink, which "is rapidly undermining the possibility for 'normal' capitalism to survive, over the medium run of the next 20–30 years." Carbon emissions from burning the fossil fuels that power capitalist industry and agriculture are overflowing the sink that the world's carbon-absorbing atmosphere, forests (themselves depleted through over-logging) and oceans have provided. The result — global warming — means longer and more severe droughts, extreme weather (from acute heat waves to super-storms) and aquifer depletion, all of which suppress agricultural yields. Higher levels of atmospheric carbon also lead to ocean acidification, compromising aquatic life systems and reducing the capacity of those systems to fix carbon. As the sink overflows with greenhouse gases and other pollutants, the tap, ironically, begins to run dry: agricultural productivity (cheap food) erodes and high-grade oil gets depleted. The consequent resort to tar-sands and other forms of "extreme oil" is increasingly more costly and creates even greater carbon emissions and ecological risk. The treadmill of production spins out of control.[22]

Viewing the system through an ecological lens, we see capitalism as embedded within the web of life, with implications that now stare us in the face. Corporate power harnesses natural processes, including labour processes, for the pursuit of private wealth. It relies whenever it can on Cheap Nature to underwrite and subsidize profitability, partly by externalizing costs. In the most recent half-century, capitalism has scaled up to such an extent that it is now in what William Rees of the University of British Columbia has called "ecological overshoot": capitalism's ecological footprint exceeds the carrying capacity of the ecosystem. This is evident in a deepening crisis whose signature symptom is global warming, which is primarily the result of two centuries of unmitigated and exponentially increasing carbon emissions.[23]

CORPORATE POWER AND "FOSSIL CAPITAL"

At the centre of this crisis is corporate power over "fossil capital," the "cheap energy" that has enabled capitalism to incorporate the "buried sunshine" of millions of years of fossilized life forms into a growth machine that now threatens the sustainability of human civilization. In this instance, corporate power resides in control over energy flows. Indeed, as historian Andreas Malm argues, "power" has a dual meaning: it is "a force of nature, a current of energy, a measure of work" and "a relation between humans, an authority, a structure of domination." Since "*all* economic activities are ultimately a matter of energy conversion," the biophysical and social forms of power have been closely entwined in all class societies. But in pre-industrial society, the dominant class's biophysical power base lay in appropriating the flow of solar energy (and energy flows of wind and water), along with the animate energy of humans and draught animals. The rise of coal-fuelled steam power in the Industrial Revolution made vast quantities of buried sunshine available to capitalists, dramatically augmenting their control of biophysical power and strengthening their social power over labour.[24]

It is no accident that corporate power emerged in the nineteenth century, along with the exponential growth associated with turning carbon energy into commodities(fossil capital). The quantum leap in energy harnessed into production is what enabled large, capital-intensive corporations. These corporations began to reshape capitalism, as we shall see, near the end of the nineteenth century. From the coal mines, railways and steel mills of that era to contemporary oil fields, energy infrastructures, manufacturing and other industries tied in with fossil-fuel energy (including industrialized agriculture), capitalism in Canada has relied on the transformation of increasing quantities of fossilized carbon into kinetic energy. The same is true globally. Geographer Richard Heede has shown that between 1751 and 2010 just ninety "carbon major" companies contributed 63 percent of total global greenhouse gas emissions. Half of those emissions occurred after 1986. A more recent study by Paul Griffin found that between 1988 and 2015 the top twenty-five carbon major companies accounted for a staggering 51 percent of global industrial greenhouse gas emissions. And through these years fossil fuel corporations benefited from massive government subsidies that, according to the International Monetary Fund, amounted to $5.3 trillion in 2015 alone.[25]

In view of the key role of fossil capital as a source of both corporate power and of climate crisis, globally and in Canada, many of our examples throughout this book are drawn from this sector. However, as this book's opening scenario suggests, the negative impact of corporate power is social as much as it is ecological. Poverty, homelessness and housing crises, malnutrition and other symptoms of social injustice are as intrinsic to capitalism as is ecological degradation.

THE ANATOMY OF CAPITALIST SOCIETY

Capitalists derive their power from capitalism's unique anatomy. First, their power over workers and society rests in control over production and the economy, and control over the economic surplus created when goods and services are made and consumed. They have direct power over other people. But, their power over others is also indirect (what some called "mediated"). This indirect power rests on the ways capitalists, individually and as a whole (as a class), can influence and have power over the political system and within what is called "civil society." As shown in Figure 1.2, the anatomy is distinctive in two ways: (1) the institutional separation of the economic from the political, and (2) the importance of civil society as a field of activity between the economy and the state.

Figure 1.2. Capitalist societies have a distinct anatomy

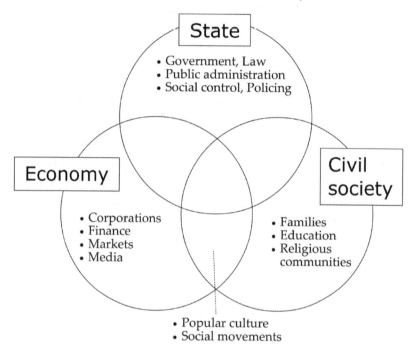

In previous societies there was no formal separation of economic and political structures. Feudal lords, for instance, owned the principal means of production in pre-industrial Europe — the land — and exploited the serfs who worked it. But, they also exercised political sovereignty over their territory and their subjects. The power to appropriate the economic surplus was interwoven with the coercive power of the state to enforce obedience. In capitalism (which emerged from European feudalism between the sixteenth and nineteenth centuries) this unity is undone. Political theorist Ellen Wood points out that the power to exploit and appropriate is transferred to a separate sphere, "the economy," and is organized around markets. Political power becomes lodged in another sphere: the state. This means that, in the words of sociologist Fred Block, "the ruling class does not rule," at least not directly. Notwithstanding such prominent outliers as billionaire capitalist and U.S. President Donald Trump, under capitalism, political leadership is distinct from economic leadership.[26]

Moreover, the capitalist state is not just coercive. Within capitalist democracies like Canada, the state is said to represent the will of citizens, constructed as a "common interest." Yet the state is structurally dependent on the economy run by capitalists as the source of its revenues. So, the "common interest" it constructs must accord with the core capitalist interest in maintaining an economy that serves their interest in unlimited profit. All this means that, besides exercising a monopoly over the use of force (including taxation) within its territory, various agencies of the state devise and implement policies to incentivize capitalist accumulation while dispensing concessions to subordinates. Such measures as minimum wages, public pensions and socialized health care — all implemented in Canada in the 1960s in response to pressure from below — serve to make the system look fair by easing the burdens on the majority of workers/citizens. Political sociologist Bob Jessop has summarized the fine balance this entails:

> The modern state's activities are said to require a healthy and growing (or at least profitable) economy – which ties political programmes to economic imperatives. Subordinate classes can secure material concessions only within this constraint: if profitability is threatened, concessions must be reversed. In periods of crisis, state dependence on continued private accumulation may even reinforce the power of capital where alternative economic imaginaries are weak and resistance is disorganized. Yet capital cannot press its economic advantages too far without undermining the state's political legitimacy, which in normal conditions requires respect for the law and for public opinion.

James O'Connor has surmised that, within corporate capitalism, the state combines the functions of coercion, accumulation and legitimation.[27]

In the twilight of European feudalism, French King Louis XIV infamously declared, "L'État, c'est moi" ("I am the State"). Such a statement could never be made within a capitalist democracy. Far from a unified agent, the state is a vast, complex terrain of struggle. But the political playing field is substantially sloped in favour of the capitalist class. Not only do state revenues depend on accumulation, but state agencies, including government, comprise an unequal structure of representation. Financial capitalists, dominant in the economic realm, are represented within the state through the Department of Finance (as well as the Treasury Board and Bank of Canada), which holds the pre-eminent position within the wider policy network. Subordinate social interests are also represented, but on the margins, including labour (Ministry of Labour) and colonized peoples (Indian Affairs and Northern Development). As political scientist Rianne Mahon summarizes:

> These [institutions] within the state ... act as the means through which the state is able to "hear" and formulate a response to the issues ... Yet just as the relations among these forces are unequal, so too does the quality and form of their representation within the state vary; the structure of representation is *unequal*.[28]

In practice, corporate power and state power entail a "*partnership between two different, separate forces,* linked to each other by many threads, yet each with their own sphere of concerns." They depend on each other, and through "revolving doors" leaders move between the two sectors. The "power bloc" — those in core positions of economic and political power — includes both state and capitalist leadership, though it can sometimes be complemented by other interest groups.[29]

The third component of capitalist society's anatomy is "civil society." There, people with their diverse needs, capacities, identities and interests sustain themselves and each other, within families, schools, religious communities, voluntary associations, trade unions, social movements, political parties and more. From the standpoint of the capitalist economy, much of what happens in civil society *reproduces* the labour-power that workers sell to capitalists for a wage. This terminology may sound strange. Karl Marx himself viewed labour-power as a most "peculiar commodity" in two senses. As we have seen, it is the unique source of more value than it is worth (i.e. surplus value). But also, unlike other commodities in a capitalist system, labour-power is not an object. It is inseparable from human beings themselves. Thus labour power is (re)produced as workers maintain their lives, both on a daily basis and across generations. By the same token, civil society (along with the state) is a key site where the dominant position of the capitalist class is also reproduced, as we shall see in Chapter 6.[30]

The central institution in these processes is the family. For the capitalist class, wealth is inherited through families, thereby reproducing the dominant class across generations (see Box 1.2). Children born to wealthy parents grow up rich. Very few members of the capitalist class come from humble backgrounds. Along with the transmission of wealth, the culture, ideology and values of the dominant class are transmitted through socialization processes centred initially in the family and later reinforced within elite private schools. Meanwhile, for workers, the family has traditionally been a site of unpaid domestic labour — housework and childcare — which reproduces labour-power, daily and intergenerationally. The predominant assignment of these activities to women has been a continuing source of gender inequity. This is evident in the so-called "traditional" model of the "upper middle class" families in which the male breadwinner pursues a professional/managerial career while the female homemaker engages in the labour of care. As feminist sociologist Dorothy Smith observes:

> The interests of the wife are held to be intimately bound up with her husband's career. In various ways she is expected to support him morally and socially as well as through the ways her domestic labour ensures both his ordinary physical well being and his proper presentation of self.

Lacking the wealth of capitalists, other families strive to inculcate in their children the capacities and sensibilities needed to get ahead in a world dominated by corporate capital. And although twenty-first century Canada is in some ways less gender-stratified than it was when Dorothy Smith's analysis was published in 1985, her basic observation on this issue still has relevance:

> Children progressively become the object of parental work, particularly the work of mothers, aimed at creating a definite kind of person with distinct communicative skills in speech and writing and with capacities to take advantage of an educational process through which boys will have access to career-structured

occupations and girls will have access to men with career-struc-
tured occupations.[31]

Other aspects of civil society are also linked into the state and to capitalists. Education — the major institution of socialization after the family
— is wholly or partly state-funded, and a good deal of schooling is adapted
to corporate needs for various kinds of skilled, qualified labour. From its

---

**BOX 1.2. THE IRVING FAMILY:
FOUR GENERATIONS OF CAPITALISTS**

The Irving family represents a concentration of corporate power in the
Maritime Provinces that stretches over four generations. They are best
known for their oil and gas branch, Irving Oil, that, among other activities,
operates the St. John, New Brunswick, oil refinery, the largest such operation
in Canada and the largest contributor to New Brunswick's economy. The
other branch of the family business, J.D. Irving Ltd., New Brunswick's
biggest private employer, is a conglomerate active in forestry, pulp and
paper, transportation, shipbuilding and more.

K.C. Irving, who first expanded the business, was the son of local
Bouctouche, New Brunswick, capitalist J.D. Irving, owner of a sawmill, a
general store, a lumber business and a farm. K.C. started his own capitalist
operation, building from a single gas station to a Canada-wide empire
spanning the whole chain of production. He also took over and widely
expanded his father's business. At K.C.'s death in 1992, his three sons, J.K.,
Arthur and Jack, each took ownership of part of the family operation. Jack
passed away in 2010 and now his eldest son, James K., representing the
fourth generation of Irving capitalists, took over his share of the business.

Over the course of almost a century of family-centred accumulation, the
Irving empire has spanned large swaths of the economy in New Brunswick
and the Maritimes. On the basis of their economic power, they were able
to secure political leverage with the provincial and federal governments.
Their influence also spread through their ownership of all three of New
Brunswick's English-language daily newspapers, as well as of eighteen of
the province's twenty-five weeklies and three radio stations. In line with
the tradition set by K.C. Irving, members of the family keep their business
activities private, and their control of the media has allowed them to contain
public criticism over the years.[32]

nineteenth century origins onward, formal education has been in part "an attempt to domesticate the working class" by teaching not only marketable skills but also time-discipline: "the ordering of work and domestic life around scheduled regularity and the principle of using time efficiently." Political parties are creatures of civil society, yet electoral successes bring them into parliament and even government. Mass media and social media are largely organized as profit-seeking corporations, although consumption of and participation in media often occur in civil society. These examples show how economy, state and civil society are intermeshed. We therefore need to see corporate power as both *direct* (capitalists and their accumulation strategies directly dominate the economy) and *mediated* through the state and the organizations and practices of civil society. A key issue, taken up in Chapter 6, is how corporate power reaches, via a panoply of relations, into political and civil society.[33]

Civil society is not simply a field in which the class positions of capitalists and workers are reproduced. Viewed not from the standpoint of capital accumulation but more broadly, civil society is pierced with social struggles for the hearts and minds of the people. Corporate influence, through media, advertising, business-funded think tanks and many other agencies, is endemic. Yet corporate rule does not go unchallenged. Various forms of counter-power, grounded in resistance or opposition to corporate and state power, have also arisen. In capitalist democracies like Canada, countervailing powers of social movements — from feminism and environmentalism to Indigenous and labour movements — have contested and even checked the powers of both state and capital. In our concluding chapter we consider some of these countervailing powers and the alternatives they pose to corporate rule. But at this point it is time to examine the development of corporate capitalism in Canada.

Chapter 2

FROM THE FUR TRADE TO BIG OIL

The Making of Corporate Power

CANADA IS A SETTLER-CAPITALIST SOCIETY

So far, we have sketched the basic terrain of corporate-capitalist society, noting that this way of life is unjust and ecologically disastrous. How did Canada develop along these lines? As with all big historical questions, the answer is complex. Important to the answer is the fact that Canada is a settler-capitalist society. This means that Canadian capitalism developed through a long (and continuing) process of colonization. Indigenous communities have lived in what is now called Canada for thousands of years, but they were systematically dispossessed of their lands and made into second-class people:

> Colonization is not only about physical occupation of someone else's land but also about the appropriation of others' political authority, cultural self-determination, economic capacity, and strategic location. That is, colonization is a profoundly exploitative relationship to the benefit of one at the expense of the Other.[1]

In this, Canada shares a similar history with the U.S., Australia, New Zealand, Israel, South Africa and Zimbabwe, although in the last two cases the European settlers never constituted a majority of the population and lost political power in recent years. The first colonization of what became

Eastern Canada was conducted by France. From 1608 to 1756, 10,000 settlers arrived (a very small number compared to the estimated population of Indigenous peoples in the northeast at that time). British colonization of what became British Columbia began in 1778. Britain and France competed for control in North America in the eighteenth century. With the 1763 Treaty of Paris, Britain gained control of New France, setting up a double colonization of both Indigenous nations and the people of New France. British dominance shaped the composition of Canada's capitalist class and of its corporate elite well into the late twentieth century. In his 1965 book *The Vertical Mosaic*, sociologist John Porter examined the consequences of this historical pattern. He reported that economic and political power in Canada was overwhelmingly held by those of British descent. A few years later, Sheilagh and Henry Milner wrote that

> an external monopoly, the Anglo-Canadian and American elites, control the Quebec economy. … It re-invests its economic surplus to expand its own enterprises, thereby reinforcing the monopoly structure, for new, smaller companies cannot afford to compete with it. But more importantly, it robs the society of the funds which could be used to produce social necessities such as public housing and adequate medical facilities.[2]

Canada's corporate elite has become more multicultural since the 1950s and 1960s, with Francophone and various ethnic minorities (mainly of European background) joining its ranks. With the transnational expansion of "home grown" Québécois corporations such as Québecor, SNC-Lavalin and Bombardier, Québec has become a full-fledged capitalist society itself. But what has not changed is the exclusion of Indigenous people from economic power, which is a symptom of both ongoing colonization and the desire by many Indigenous communities to maintain collectivist ways of life that are radically different from corporate capitalism.[3]

At the core of colonization is the dispossession of land from its original occupants. In fact, capitalism was founded on dispossession in two ways. First, in what became capitalism's European heartland, peasants were dispossessed from the land by a series of state-mandated "enclosures" from the fifteenth to the nineteenth centuries. Enclosure eliminated "the commons" (land possessed and managed in common) and assigned ownership of land to an emergent class of capitalist farmers. The dispossessed peasantry became workers, who were compelled to work for wages in order to gain access to subsistence, and who eventually became fully integrated into the new capitalist economy, losing their link to the land.

Second, in Canada and other settler-capitalist societies, it was Indigenous peoples who were dispossessed. As Dene scholar Glen Coulthard writes, "these formative acts of violent *dispossession*" set the stage for modern capitalism "by tearing Indigenous societies, peasants, and other small-scale, self-sufficient agricultural producers from the source of their livelihood — *the land.*" Land grabbing was foundational to "the violent transformation of noncapitalist forms of life into capitalist ones." But in contrast to the dispossessed peasants who were reshaped into Europe's working class (some of whom settled in Canada), Indigenous nations were displaced onto reserves that comprised a tiny fraction of their earlier land base. They were effectively dispossessed without being integrated into capitalism as workers. This rendered them marginalized and dominated by the Canadian state. The Indian Act (1876), according to Kwakwaka'wakw writer Gord Hill, gave the federal government "complete control over the economic, social, and political affairs of Native communities." The Act is still the basis of Indigenous-state relations.[4]

Although the intent of colonization was always to assimilate "by destroying Aboriginal political systems and social organization, religion and the remnants of once-viable economies," Indigenous communities proved resilient and resistant. Unlike the former European peasantry, and despite the trauma of residential schools (first established in the 1890s and finally closed in 1996), Indigenous peoples across Canada maintained their deep ties to the land, which is the basis for an alternative way of life. Today, they press land claims against the Canadian state and often come into direct conflict with mining, fossil fuel and other corporations interested in using Indigenous land as a tap or a sink. Colonization is an ongoing process involving a confluence of state and corporate power, against which Indigenous peoples and their allies continue to struggle. Focusing on the link between colonization and capitalism means high-lighting the partnership of corporate capitalists and the colonizing state, which has been integral to the formation of Canada.[5]

ESTABLISHING SETTLER CAPITALISM

We can distinguish three periods of Canadian capitalist development, each with its own confluence of corporate and state power. In the first, from the seventeenth century to roughly the mid-1800s, European colonists engaged in extensive trade with Indigenous peoples (particularly in fur), and established the premises for settler capitalism. The Hudson's Bay Company (HBC), now the oldest corporation in the English-speaking world, was the leading colonizing force in this period. Established in 1670, the HBC served effectively both as a state body (sovereign over the land it controlled) and as one of the first giant corporations in the world. Its royal charter initially granted the company a monopoly over 40 percent of what eventually became Canada, which is one of the biggest land-grabs in history. According to the HBC Archives, King Charles "believed that the land was his to give because no other Christian monarch had claimed it." No Indigenous nations, who physically occupied the land, were consulted.[6]

Within the HBC, power was highly centralized yet delegated in part to local supervisors. A group of wealthy London-based capitalists owned the company's shares and elected the governance committee, including the Governor, who was both Chairman of the Board and political authority. The actual work was done by trappers and traders, typically in collaboration with Indigenous communities who often exchanged furs for blankets. As the frontier extended westward, the HBC built trails and fortified trading posts. These became the infrastructure for colonial settlement in the nineteenth century. The HBC's empire also came to include what is now British Columbia. Victoria, for example, was established in 1843 as a fortified HBC trading post that displaced the Songhees village directly adjacent to it. In 1849, the British Crown granted all of Vancouver Island to the Company, another massive land-grab executed without consultation with Indigenous peoples. Within a very few years of the establishment of Fort Victoria, former HBC supervisor James Dunsmuir, soon to become B.C.'s richest capitalist, controlled extensive coal mining centred in Nanaimo, a gift of Cheap Nature from the Crown.[7]

By mid-century the HBC's business strategy, which favoured preservation of the forests that supported fur-bearing animals over the clearing of land and settlement, had become out dated. In 1863, a new group of

London capitalists with interests in railways, land development and banking took control of HBC. Their objective was opening up HBC land for settlement and mining and building a transcontinental railway to British Columbia. By 1870, in a Deed of Surrender, the HBC ceded its claim to Rupert's Land and the Northwest Territories, which by then comprised three-quarters of the landmass of contemporary Canada. The HBC did this in exchange for money and substantial tracts of prime land around its trading posts (some of which became major cities like Winnipeg and Edmonton) and in the so-called fertile belt, from the Red River to the Rockies. As historical geographer Frank Tough concludes:

> Eventually, the settler replaced the fur trader, but the owners of the HBC realized their interest in the fertile belt. Between 1905 and 1922, the Company's dividend rate ranged from 20 to 50 percent. These large dividends were supported by land sales. Although Native peoples were kept at a subsistence level, the HBC accumulated capital. Between 1891 and 1930 the HBC's land earnings netted profits of $96,366,021, a far cry from the £2 million invested in 1863.[8]

Coinciding with Confederation and the creation of Manitoba and B.C. as provinces, this first massive restructuring of corporate capitalism opened the West to full-fledged colonization and capitalist development.

THE EMERGENCE OF CORPORATE CAPITALISM IN THE LATE NINETEENTH CENTURY

The second period of Canadian capitalist development was now underway, with extensive settlement in Ontario and Quebec and accelerating displacement of Indigenous peoples. The basic elements of industrial capitalism were quickly developing, including

- an agricultural surplus to feed urban populations,
- a proletarian class of mostly immigrant wage-workers in the towns and cities,
- small-scale manufactories,
- large-scale transportation infrastructure in the form of canals and the first railways,

- and an integrated home market and financial system, with the first bank, Bank of Montreal, chartered in 1817.

Railways were particularly important, both in knitting places together and in absorbing massive quantities of industrial products such as steel and coal. Similarly to the HBC, railway corporations fused economic and political power and, in particular, the coercive power of the state, which was delegated to them. Historian H.C. Pentland noted that in mid-nineteenth century Canada private railway corporations assumed the right of the state to keep and direct their own police forces. Moreover, when, in response to labour unrest, "the manager of a large private corporation demanded troops, officials learned not to ask whether they were needed, but rushed a force off as soon as possible."[9]

It was in this period, particularly in the era of the National Policy (beginning in 1879 and continuing well into the early decades of the twentieth century) that corporate capitalism was consolidated in Canada. Led by the dominant capitalists and politicians of the late nineteenth century, the National Policy contained three key provisions:

- construction of a national railway,
- immigration and settlement of western Canada,
- and high customs fees (tariffs) on imported manufactured goods.

These measures worked in unison to enlarge a "home market" within which capital could accumulate at a rapid pace. The railway and tariffs not only stimulated local industry. They in effect secured the territory of Canada for domestically based business, creating an east-west transportation corridor while making imported manufactured goods more expensive. Meanwhile, immigration and settlement policy brought fresh labour-power to industry and accelerated the colonizing project. By the close of the century, prairie farmers were buying supplies from eastern-based manufacturers and supplying cheap food to eastern cities, lowering the cost of labour-power and thus boosting profits.[10]

Given the resource-richness of the Canadian landmass, the consolidation of capitalism clearly benefited from what Jason Moore calls the "four cheaps" — labour-power, food, energy and natural resources. The low cost of these four basic economic inputs boosted profits by keeping the cost of production down. Cheap food and cheap labour-power went hand-in-hand, particularly in a context where minimum wages were unheard of and labour unions were just beginning to stir. Cheap raw materials and energy came out of land that was grabbed from Indigenous communities, and then bestowed by the state upon mining, lumber and railway magnates. These practices redistributed wealth upwards from Indigenous nations and workers to capitalists, and at the same time transformed the landscape. Canada has recently been identified as the world leader in deforestation, a process that contributes to global warming by reducing the capacity of forests to fix carbon through photosynthesis. But extensive deforestation in Canada goes back to the nineteenth century, when lumber production became a leading industrial sector. Unhampered by any state-mandated restrictions on allowable cut or logging practices, the industry expanded constantly, clearing new land as its "sustained attack on the forest" lowered the quantity and quality of available timber.[11]

The partnership of nascent corporate capitalists and the state was a close one, to say the very least. Railways were by far the most capital-intensive mega-projects of the era, and many members of the Dominion Parliament were railway promoters. As muckraking historian Gustavus Myers wrote in 1913, "The public finances have been placed at the disposal of railway promoters in three principal forms. Cash subsidies, comprising outright cash or loans has been one method; land grants, another; and guarantees of bonds a third." By Myers's reckoning, the totals amounted to 56 million acres of land, $244 million in cash subventions (mostly outright donations) and $245 million in bond guarantees. Since members of Parliament were mostly capitalists (until 1917 only non-Indigenous men who owned property could vote or hold office in Canada), it is not surprising that they gave themselves various railway charters and concessions: "The chief beneficiaries often were the foremost members — men who were leaders, or who evolved into leaders of political parties, or who became Cabinet Ministers or Prime Ministers."[12]

The most prominent of these business/political leaders was Donald Alexander Smith, also known as Lord Strathcona (1820–1914). A Member of Parliament (1871–1880 and 1887–1896), a Peer in the British House of Lords (from 1897) and Canadian High Commissioner to the U.K. from 1896 until his death in 1914, Smith's career began in 1842 with the HBC, where he administered the fur trade in Labrador. Promoted to manager of the Company's eastern activities in 1868, he negotiated the HBC's Deed of Surrender and thereafter became involved in HBC land sales while developing interests in railways. He became a director of the Bank of Montreal in 1872, and he was made vice-president in 1882 and president in 1887. Smith's elite positions in Canada's emerging corporate economy enabled him to accumulate capital in the form of corporate shares, and by 1889, as the principal shareholder in HBC, he was elected its governor. He was appointed a director of the Canadian Pacific Railway (CPR) in 1883 and drove the "last spike" in a ceremony at Craigellachie, B.C., on November 7, 1885.

Figure 2.1. Donald Smith driving the
last spike of the Canadian Pacific Railway[13]

With investments and directorships in a raft of corporations – from Dominion Coal Company and Canadian Salt Company to the *Manitoba Free Press* and both Montreal Trust and Royal Trust, Smith was the leading corporate capitalist of his time. His career spanned the entire formative era of Canadian corporate capitalism, and in his final decade his business interests reached internationally to Persia (now Iran) and the Indian subcontinent, as he became the first Chairman and the largest individual shareholder in the Anglo-Persian Oil Company — the forerunner to BP, a position he held until his death. Fossil capital was beginning to internationalize and to transition from King Coal to Big Oil, and the leading light of Canada's corporate community was at the forefront.[14]

THE MAKING OF CORPORATE CAPITALISM: KEY ELEMENTS

Donald Smith epitomized the corporate capitalists of this second era of capitalist development during the late nineteenth and early twentieth centuries. He came to occupy a central position within the emerging corporate community, directing the county's largest financial institution, its largest industrial corporation (the CPR) and its largest commercial corporation (the HBC) while also exercising political leadership. Three interrelated developments were at work here:

1. concentration and centralization, meaning fewer, and larger, companies came to dominate the entire economy;
2. integration of large-scale industrial and financial capital to form finance capital (see Box 2.1);
3. full development of the corporate form of business organization, including groups of associated capitalists.

Concentration and centralization are inevitable results of competition among capitalists. Concentration occurs as capitalists, eager to stay a step ahead of competitors, plough their profits back into enlarged production, increasing the mass of wealth they control. Centralization occurs as smaller, weaker businesses are absorbed by the stronger, leaving fewer, and larger, enterprises. Karl Marx traced both these tendencies in *Capital*, pointing to the long-range result: a form of capitalism in which free-market competition among many relatively small firms gives way to monopoly power. The decades surrounding the turn of the twentieth century witnessed the emergence of large manufacturing companies, as many smaller firms amalgamated. By 1907, according to historian Richard De Grass, "Canada was already dominated by a few large corporations." Between 1908 and 1913, an intense merger movement centralized another 229 industrial firms into the corporations that would dominate the Canadian economy throughout the rest of the century. Banks also merged, and the number of chartered banks fell from thirty-four in 1907 to twenty-two in 1914.[15]

BOX 2.1. FINANCE CAPITAL

The concept of finance capital was first used by Austrian political economist Rudolph Hilferding to designate the tight coupling he observed in early twentieth century Germany between, on the one hand, industrial corporations and the means of production they controlled — industrial capital — and, on the other hand, the vast sums of money controlled and allocated by large banks — financial capital.

As the corporate form generalized, capital became increasingly concentrated in large corporations. Industrial corporations needed access to vast pools of money to finance their expansion if they were to compete on the national scene, and eventually they had to enter the monetary sphere themselves. Conversely, financial institutions established close relations with their clients as they took an interest in overseeing their increasingly large loans and investments. This interpenetration and interdependency of financial and industrial interests came to structure a large part of the field of corporate power in Canada as well as in other core capitalist countries over the course of the twentieth century and into the twenty-first century.[16]

As for the second development, within capitalism there is a symbiotic relation between industrial capitalists and the expansion of the credit system. As the scale of economic activities grows, a company's expansion cannot be funded from its savings (retained earnings), but must be financed through credit. At the same time, the main sources of credit, financial institutions, amass vast funds that must be invested in profitable ventures. The concentration and centralization into a relatively small number of very large companies creates a "community of interest" between the top industrialists in need of financing and the top bankers and financiers in need of investment outlets. Political economist Rudolf Hilferding noted:

> A circle of people emerges who, thanks to their own capital resources or to the concentrated power of outside capital which they represent (in the case of bank directors), become members of the boards of directors of numerous corporations. There develops in this way a kind of personal union, on one side among the various corporations themselves, and on the other, between the

corporations and the bank; and the common ownership interest which is thus formed among the various companies must necessarily exert a powerful influence upon their policies.[17]

This "fusion" of the major financial and industrial concerns created strong interdependencies between big industry and high finance. It is reflected not only in relations between capitalist corporations (bank loans to industry and shareholdings in corporations, for example) but in the governance of large corporations. Again, Donald Smith came to personify this integration in the early decades of Canadian corporate capitalism, with his extensive investments and directorships in leading corporations. But Smith was simply an illustrious instance of a wider phenomenon throughout what became the advanced capitalist world: a financial-industrial elite of the most powerful capitalists, forming the leading edge of the capitalist class. What Hilferding noticed and what Donald Smith exemplified was the tendency in advanced capitalism for the forms of capital (industry, finance, trade) to become functionally interwoven under the sway of a financial-industrial elite. This elite's ownership and/ or control of key blocs and pools of financial capital would afford them unprecedented economic power.

This brings us to the third development in the making of corporate capitalism: the adoption by leading businesses of the "corporate form." Before the closing decades of the nineteenth century, corporations were relatively rare entities, and they were typically created by special charters, as was the HBC. Capitalist businesses were structured as proprietorships (one owner) or partnerships (multiple owners), and they did not issue shares that could be bought and sold. But as the modern credit system developed, new forms of capitalist property and new markets for trading titles to property emerged. Limited-liability corporations appeared, in which many capitalists can buy shares that entitle them to part of the venture's profits. As this new mode of organizing business gained importance in the second half of the nineteenth century, stock exchanges on which corporations' shares could be traded were set up. The Toronto Stock Exchange opened in 1861, followed by Montreal's in 1874. In the interim the Canadian colonies adopted the newly-minted provision for "limited liability," under British company law, in 1862. Prior to limited liability, each investor was personally liable, without limit, for a company's debt, meaning that "a person risked financial ruin simply by owning shares in a company." Advocated with obvious self-interest by business leaders, limited liability immunized investors against claims beyond the amounts they had invested in a company. This new form of organization thereby allowed company owners to transfer the risk onto their financial backers, and also to externalize a large part of the social and environmental costs to the public, who has to foot the bill for destructive impacts of bankrupt companies.[18]

The corporate form — the parceling of corporate ownership into many tradeable shares offering limited liability to investors — accelerated centralization. It also expanded the scale of production by enabling groups of capitalists to pool their investments into the "social capital" of directly associated stockholders, such as Donald Smith and his cronies at the HBC, CPR and Bank of Montreal. Finance capitalists like Smith, often operating in collaboration, were able to control enormous quantities of capital, with limited liability and the ability to divest from a company at will. The upshot was a massive increase in speculation and corruption. Marx observed the contradiction in this. As capital became more concentrated and centralized, production became more "socialized": meaning it was undertaken by vast workforces within complex divisions of labour requiring high levels of cooperation and coordination. Capital itself was, within the bourgeoisie, becoming "social." Firms were no longer the private possessions of individuals but the collaborative projects of associated capitalists, and capitalists could buy and sell corporate shares at will in pursuit of maximum profit. Yet the class divide between capitalists and workers remained intact (and arguably deepened, with the super-affluence of the emerging corporate elite). Moreover, the corporate form of organization intensified capital's tendency toward centralization. As Marx put it, "Since property here exists in the form of stock, its movement and transfer become purely a result of gambling on the stock exchange, where the little fish are swallowed by the sharks and the lambs by the stock-exchange wolves."[19]

By the early twentieth century, the corporation had become the dominant form of business organization in Canada. It is important to grasp how this form reconfigured, yet reproduced, the capitalist class as a ruling class. The key to this reconfiguration lies in the governance structure of the corporation. As Roderick Wood points out:

The structure of a corporation consists of shareholders, directors and officers. Corporations are subject to a centralized management structure in that the authority to manage the business is allocated to the directors. Directors are responsible for supervision of the business activities, the appointment of the officers and for broad policy decisions. Corporate officers are delegated responsibility for the day-to-day operations of the business.

Although shareholders, directors and officers (the top executive team) play distinct roles, an individual may act in multiple capacities; Donald Smith's occupation of all three roles at the HBC and Bank of Montreal in the late nineteenth century is but one example. And although shareholders have no direct control over business decisions, they do elect the board of directors at the annual general meeting.[20]

The election of directors takes place on the basis of one share, one vote. From a capitalist standpoint, this makes sense: the more shares one owns, the more say one should have in how the corporation functions. But the one share, one vote rule differs radically from the basic principle of democratic decision-making of one person, one vote. In practice, the same stock-exchange wolves that, in Marx's vivid imagery, swallow the lambs also hold sway in electing the corporation's directors. That is to say, the shareholders who own the most shares (or a single dominant shareholder) are typically in a position to determine the composition of the board of directors, where the authority to manage the business resides. This enables major shareholders to effectively control entire corporations through owning strategic blocs of shares. They thereby control the capital of all the smaller investors in the same companies, who are effectively disenfranchised.

Putting these three elements of corporate capitalism together, we see that at the turn of the nineteenth century a combination of capital concentration and centralization, capital integration (the fusion of big industry and finance), and the adoption of the corporate form by major companies brought into being a financial-industrial elite: a small group of finance capitalists who controlled Canada's major businesses. If Donald Smith was iconic, he was not alone, nor was his coterie of Montreal-based capitalists controlling the HBC, CPR, Bank of Montreal and other corporations the only financial group dominating Canada's corporate landscape. In

Toronto, the same three processes of concentration/centralization, capital integration and corporatization produced a financial group that in 1906 included Senator George Cox's Canada Life Assurance, the Canadian Bank of Commerce, Dominion Iron and Steel, and William McKenzie and Donald Mann's McKenzie Mann and Company (which controlled the forerunner to the Canadian National Railway).[21]

Nor was Canada at all exceptional. Political economist Ernest Mandel, writing in the 1960s, made the following observation:

> The same structure is discovered to exist in the majority of the capitalist countries: an handful of financial groups possessing control over a large proportion of industrial and financial activity; some 60, 125 or 200 families placed at the apex of the social pyramid, who wield their power sometimes as individuals but often as a more or less compact collective group.

By the 1920s, corporate capitalism had fully arrived in Canada. With it came a corporate elite "whose interlocking interests and corporate positions effectively fused big industry with high finance."[22]

In turn, the coming of age of corporate capitalism enabled Canada's leading finance capitalists to begin investing internationally, and, as Libby and Frank Park showed in 1962, Canadian banks established themselves, through subsidiaries, in much of the Caribbean.[23] We have already seen this tendency toward international investment in the case of Donald Smith. Not to be outdone, one of his main rivals in the division of spoils, William McKenzie, invested in Brazil, where his Brazilian Traction, Light and Power Company Limited, incorporated in 1912, came to control major hydroelectric and transportation works through the takeover of various local Brazilian firms.

This early internationalization of corporate capitalism followed the same basic logic as all capitalist investment: the quest for higher rates of profit. In effect, "surplus capital" appropriated in Canada was "exported" elsewhere, to establish or acquire businesses where higher rates of return could be realized. Again, Canada's big bourgeoisie was not alone, but was typical of other capitalist powers in establishing corporations abroad. Indeed, the internationalization of corporate capitalism is a fourth key element in its constitution. With internationalization came the phenomenon of modern imperialism. As political economist Nicolai Bukharin explained in his seminal work, *Imperialism and World Economy*,

> What we have in a "foreign" country are large sums of money,
> particularly of fixed capital, invested in gigantic constructions:
> railroads stretching over thousands of miles, very costly electric
> plants, large plantations, etc., etc. The capitalists of the exporting
> country are materially interested in "guarding" their wealth. They
> are therefore ready to go the limit in order that they may retain the
> freedom of further accumulation. ... Capital export is the most
> convenient method for the economic policy of financial groups;
> it subjugates new territories with the greatest ease.[24]

"Guarding" the investments of northern-based capitalists in the Global
South, often by resort to military force, has been a basic task for capitalist
states, both the imperialist ones in the North and local ones in the South.
By the 1920s, as political ecologist Timothy Mitchell points out, "a hand-
ful of industrialised states in the global north had brought much of the
world under the control of imperial government." Fast-forward to 2001
and the American invasion of Afghanistan, in which Canadian troops
participated. On November 26, U.S. General James "Mad Dog" Mattis
(now Secretary of Defense) declared that "the marines have landed and
we now own a piece of Afghanistan." Canadian political economist David
McNally has decoded the larger meaning of this statement: "The general's
declaration managed in a single sentence to encapsulate the very spirit of
imperialism: the idea that the world's dominant economic and military
powers can claim ownership and control of a part of the world by virtue
of military force."[25]

Canadian corporate power thus came of age on the basis of three
sources of wealth: colonization within Canada's borders (dispossessing
Indigenous peoples through expansion westward and northward) and
imperialism abroad (through the international investments of Canadian
multinationals, particularly in the western hemisphere). Alongside this
geographical expansion, capital accumulated through exploitation of
the urban proletariat that was congregating in the cities and towns of the
eastern and central settled regions. All three of these engines of accumulation and corporate power continue to have traction in the present day.

CONSOLIDATING CORPORATE POWER IN THE ERA OF ORGANIZED CAPITALISM: 1920S–1970S

This brings us to the third era in the development of corporate power. By the 1920s, as Rudolph Hilferding argued, a distinct form of organized capitalism had emerged in what we now call the Global North. The new stage "was marked by concentration and bureaucratization in production, the organization of both labor and employers into interest groups, and an activist state role in economic decisions."[26]

Advanced capitalist societies, including Canada, were increasingly structured around large bureaucratic organizations: corporations and state bodies. In Canada, trade unions, the principal organizations through which workers resist corporate power, increased their sway, particularly in the 1930s, as industrial workers in large corporations became organized. Corporate capitalists also organized themselves into industry groups, the most prominent and politically influential being the Canadian Manufacturers' Association (incorporated in 1902) and the Canadian Bankers Association (founded in 1894). These industry groups established close ties to government; indeed, the first Bank Act (1871) was essentially drafted by the Bank of Montreal, and in the early years of Confederation, the Canadian Bankers Association effectively chose the federal Minister of Finance. As corporate power became more bureaucratically organized, it began to reach in a systematic way into the political field.[27]

Meanwhile, federal and provincial governments began to intervene more extensively in attempts to manage the capitalist economy, through policies such as unemployment insurance (brought in during the Great Depression of the 1930s) and by creating crown corporations. The state had heavily subsidized the CPR and other capitalist-controlled railways, several of which were bankrupt by 1918, when the federal government amalgamated them into the publicly-owned Canadian National Railway (CNR). By 1923, as a measure of the weight of railway investment in Canadian capitalism, 60 percent of the total assets of the hundred largest non-financial companies, and almost 40 percent of all nonfinancial capital, was claimed by two corporations: CNR and CPR. State-owned telephone and electrical utilities such as SaskTel (1908) and Ontario Hydro (1906) were established beginning in the twentieth century's first decade. In the 1930s, the Canadian Broadcasting Corporation (CBC) and Air Canada were spun off from the CNR and established, and in 1938 the Bank of Canada became a federal crown corporation. These state-owned corporations would comprise a significant piece of Canada's developing corporate economy well into the late twentieth century.[28]

To these structural aspects of organized capitalism we must add the increasingly organized character of the corporate elite. This is evident in the growth of an elite network of interlocking boards of directors among Canada's leading corporations, in the first few decades of the twentieth century. We noted earlier that a corporation's board of directors is responsible for major strategic decisions and that by the early twentieth century major finance capitalists like Donald Smith and Alexander McKenzie had taken up multiple directorships in the corporations they controlled. Their multiple corporate affiliations, and those of other major corporate capitalists, created a dense network of interlocking boards and the basis for an elite corporate community. In Chapter 5 we map the contemporary Canadian corporate network as an important centre of power. Here it is sufficient to note that the era of organized capitalism brought a massive expansion and integration of the network.

Gilles Piédalue's study of the Canadian corporate network between 1900 and 1930 showed that 80 percent of the country's largest companies shared at least one director with another large company in 1900; by 1930 this had increased to 91 percent. On average, these interlocked corporations were directly linked to eight companies in 1900 and to fifteen by 1930. From 1900 to 1930, the percentage of Canadian (as opposed to foreign) directors rose from 73 to 81, indicating a consolidation of corporate power among Canada's leading capitalists. The strongest ties in the network — those carried by three or more interlocked directors — tended to be focused on the country's three major banks (Bank of Montreal, Bank of Commerce, Royal Bank) which Piédalue saw as the centres of integrated financial groups.[29]

Corporate capitalism in Canada emerged from the turbulence of the Great Depression and World War Two on a relatively strong footing, having benefited from extensive state support during the war and not having suffered the devastation experienced in Europe and Japan. This was reflected in the structure of the corporate elite. By 1946, the country's first major financial group (the legacy of Donald Smith) continued to be at the centre of the corporate power structure, but the group had grown substantially. Joining the CPR, HBC and Bank of Montreal in the dominant, Montreal-based financial group of twenty heavily interlocked companies were the Royal Bank of Canada, Sun Life and the Steel Company of Canada (Stelco).[30]

However, the much larger American state and economy emerged from the Depression and the war even stronger. Indeed, the period from 1945 to the early 1970s was a time of unrivalled American political and economic dominance within global capitalism. In the initial post-war years, with Europe and Japan in ruins and their political futures unclear, U.S.-based capitalists controlled the world's largest transnational corporations (TNCs) and banks. They accumulated enormous surpluses of capital, much of which was invested, through their subsidiaries, in Canada's high-growth economy. Canada was a prime destination for U.S.-based corporate capital because of its political stability, its proximity and its unparalleled natural resources and "Cheap Nature." This quickly elevated the level of American control over capital in Canada. By the mid-1960s, concern was growing about Canadian business' "silent surrender" to U.S.-based TNCs, as political economist Kari Levitt famously wrote.[31]

In the 1970s, a distinctive interpretation of corporate power in Canada gained influence, as numerous scholars argued that Canada's capitalist class had followed an exceptional course. Daniel Drache, R.T. Naylor, Wallace Clement and others suggested that, in contrast to the normal capitalist trajectory, Canada's corporate elite was dominated by a group of bankers and merchants (that is, traders, not producers) who aligned themselves not with local industry but with foreign and particularly American transnationals. Although the evidence we have presented so far runs against this thesis, the key issue was whether, in the post-war era, corporate power became reorganized around an alliance of Canadian bankers/merchants and foreign-based industry, presiding over a cumulative process of silent surrender and underdevelopment. Or, had Canada's corporate elite continued as in other advanced capitalist societies, with a dominant group controlling finance capital and showing the capacity to accumulate globally?[32]

The weight of evidence amassed in the 1980s and more recently strongly supports the latter interpretation:

1. Although American direct investment poured into Canada after World War Two, its expansion ebbed in the 1970s as American global hegemony weakened and as Canadian-based capitalists strengthened their control of the home market. The "silent surrender" that Kari Levitt projected as a cumulative process turned out to be confined to an era in which Canada's capitalists did not "surrender" but pursued opportunities within a U.S.-centred global regime that dominated Europe and Japan as much as Canada.

2. From the 1940s through the 1980s, the boards of leading industrial corporations and financial institutions controlled by Canadian capitalists remained tightly interlocked, forming a national corporate community and a dominant group of finance capitalists centred in Toronto and Montréal.

3. Foreign controlled companies did not participate extensively in the network of corporate interlocks. Earlier notions of an alliance of Canada's commercial bourgeoisie and U.S. TNCs (as in Clement's work) were overstated.

4. Canadian capitalists, through their own transnational corporations, quickened their investments abroad, showing a capacity not only to grow within their home market and to export goods into other national economies, but to "export capital" to the most promising locales on a transnational basis.[33]

In short, the middle to later decades of the twentieth century marked a continuation and consolidation of "organized capitalism," similar to other countries of the Global North. Changes also occurred in the structure of corporate power. From the mid-1940s to the 1970s and 1980s, the dominant, Montreal-based financial group persisted, yet several new groups emerged, which were predominantly centred in Toronto. The various groups came to include a wider swathe of large corporations, with the big banks linking across groups. The elite network thus became "increasingly integrated yet differentiated." In short, Canada's capitalist class strengthened its control of large corporations and banks and internationalized its reach through foreign investment, even as corporate giants from the U.S. and other countries also reached into Canada through their own foreign subsidiaries.[34]

FROM CLASS COMPROMISE TO NEOLIBERAL GLOBALIZATION

In Chapter 1, we wrote of the free market, a concept at the centre of the liberal ideology that legitimates capitalism as a way of life. As we have seen in this chapter, even a century ago, Canadian capitalism could not be reasonably described as organized around free markets. Large corporations already dominated the scene at the close of the nineteenth century! The organized capitalism that developed through the twentieth century concentrated economic power in the hands of a highly cohesive financial-industrial elite. The concentration of capital within a relative few giant corporations, many controlled by capitalists in Canada, others by capitalists elsewhere, put in place the basic institutional power structures that prevail to this day.

However, the organized capitalism of the post-war economic boom (mid 1940s through mid-1970s) also contributed to labour's growing strength. Labour activism led to the recognition of a new form of human rights: the right of workers to join unions and bargain collectively with employers (first recognized in Canada in 1944). As workers joined unions and as low unemployment rates improved labour's bargaining power, real wages rose. Within the logic of organized capitalism, as David Wolfe and others have pointed out, the state came to mediate a "class compromise." This meant that the struggle between labour and capital was institutionalized within a framework of industrial relations which, for three decades, created a "positive sum game" in which both parties could benefit.[35]

This policy framework is known as "Keynesian" in honour of John Maynard Keynes, the British economist who developed it during the Great Depression. Keynes argued that to avoid crisis and stagnation due to under-consumption, state managers needed to keep overall demand in the national economy buoyant. To accomplish this, policies of income redistribution through progressive taxation, generous social programs and "full employment" (keeping unemployment rates low) were implemented, adding up to the so-called Keynesian welfare state (KWS). For corporate capitalists, the KWS meant higher taxes and greater regulation, yet it held important advantages. It bought labour peace by giving workers a stake in the system, and by keeping overall demand buoyant, it supported the development of consumer capitalism as a way of life. The scourge of under-consumption — one cause of crisis — seemed beaten. In turn, mass consumption was fed by mass production, all within a state-managed national economy. This "regime of accumulation" has been called "Fordism," after the first major corporate capitalist to adopt assembly-line production, Henry Ford. In Canada, widespread adoption of assembly-line production and other productivity-enhancing innovations after World War Two created a rapidly growing economic pie to be divided between capital and labour, which kept profits high and allowed wages to grow.[36]

Yet by the mid-1970s, this paradigm was fraying, as productivity gains weakened and corporate profits declined in the face of continuing pressure for higher wages and salaries. Large corporations, dominating markets, were able to pass cost increases onto consumers. Workers reacted by pushing for higher wages to compensate for higher prices, resulting in hyperinflation, a fall in the actual value of money and what it can buy. By the late 1970s and early 1980s, Canadian capitalism (along with its counterparts in the Global North) was facing a new scourge: "stagflation," which is the combination of inflation due to rising wages and prices and stagnation due to lower profits. For the state, stagflation meant lower revenues from taxation yet higher costs due to both inflation and increased need, in a stagnant economy, for social assistance. And that combination meant government budget deficits and rising state debt.[37]

It was in this context that the corporate elite in Canada and elsewhere mobilized politically around a project of "neoliberal globalization." Corporate capitalists pressed successfully in the 1980s for a new policy framework that would restore profitability by weakening the power of unions, curtailing social programs, reducing taxes (especially on businesses and the wealthy) and facilitating the further growth of international business. In Canada, the centrepiece of neoliberal policy has been "free trade," initially with the U.S. (1988), then extended to Mexico (1994) and more recently to the European Union. The neoliberal regime deregulated markets and reduced social provisioning, effectively redistributing wealth and income upward, based on a framework of continental, and increasingly transnational, accumulation.

As corporate capital became more transnational, the logic of organized capitalism, which had come to feature an active role for the state in managing the economy, gave way to a new logic where states removed limitations on the international movement of capital. Under the logic of "disorganized capitalism," instead of striving to promote its *capitalists* within a buoyant home market, the state's role in accumulation is focused around promoting its *territory* as an attractive site for investment that might otherwise locate elsewhere. This means keeping wages, taxes and other deductions from potential profit low.[38]

Economist Jordan Brennan has charted some key trends in the shift from the organized capitalism of the post-war class compromise to the "disorganized capitalism" and neoliberal globalization of recent decades. During the post-war class compromise, the early-twentieth century pattern of extremely concentrated corporate capital was eroded, only to be re-established in the late twentieth century. In 1961, the sixty largest corporations listed on the Toronto Stock Exchange (the TSX 60), claimed 35 percent of aggregated net profits of all firms in Canada. This already amounted to an enormous concentration of capital. But the figure grew to an astonishing 60 percent by 2010, indicating that most of the surplus produced by Canadian workers was captured as the profit of just sixty corporations (Figure 2.2). This increase occurred with the turn to neoliberalism and the signing of continental "free trade" deals in 1989 and 1994, despite the fact that the total number of firms had grown from 153,000 in 1965 to more than 1.3 million in 2009. By 2010, *most of the profits of 1.3 million companies were claimed by just 60 giant corporations.* The market value of these same giant corporations now accounted for most of the value of all 2,100 companies whose shares are listed on the Toronto Stock Exchange. "Total market capitalization" is the value of all shares of all firms listed on the stock exchange. In 1956, the top sixty corporations accounted for 29 percent of the total market capitalization of the Toronto Stock Exchange. By 2010, they claimed 60 percent, confirming that a few dozen giant corporations now "dominate the Canadian political economy, driving the accumulation process."[39]

David Macdonald of the Canadian Centre for Policy Alternatives has shown that the same pattern of concentrated ownership applies to people. In 2012, the richest Canadian residents, representing just 0.0002 per cent of the population, owned wealth equivalent to the poorest 34 per cent of the population (11.4 million people). Much of the wealth of these select few consists in concentrated corporate shareholdings, placing many of

Figure 2.2. Share of the largest 60 companies in the Canadian economy[40]

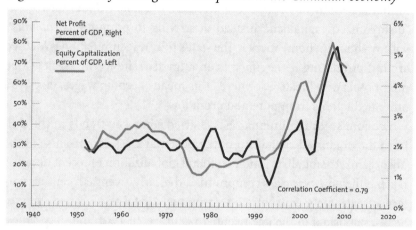

them in a position to control or influence decision-making in leading Canadian corporations.[41]

Even more remarkable is the close relationship, since the 1950s, between the concentration of corporate capital and the extent of income inequality. Between 1950 and 2007, the average profit of the TSX 60 grew from representing 234 times the average profit for all firms in Canada to 14,278 times the average profit. This indicates ever-increasing capital concentration through high rates of accumulation by giant firms that, as we have seen, claim most of the total surplus value. The share of total income going to the top 0.1 percent of income earners declined in the era of the kws, from three percent to below two percent in the early 1980s. But as neoliberal globalization gained traction, the top 0.1 percent's share increased dramatically, reaching five percent in the mid-2000s (Figure 2.3). Especially since the early 1990s, the *concentration of corporate capital* has closely tracked the *concentration of income* in an elite few, producing an "unprecedented concentration of both income and corporate power." Jordan Brennan draws an additional conclusion, noting that dominant corporations are, unlike smaller firms, in a position to shape and even "make" prices, which is partly why they claim so much profit:

> These large firms effectively exist, then, in a separate political economy than the majority of small- and medium-sized firms who are price-takers and are relatively powerless. Large firms

are price-shapers and price-makers. They have a visible hand in shaping not only the industrial process, but the distribution of income, and therefore the growth or reduction of income inequality as well.[42]

Figure 2.3. Concentration of capital and concentration of income[43]

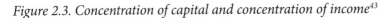

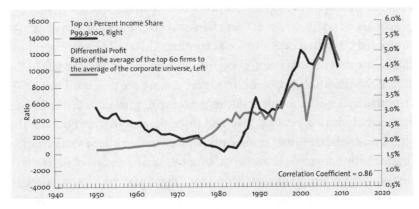

BOX 2.2. BREAD PRICE-FIXING AGREEMENT

At the end of 2017, Loblaws, Canada's largest supermarket, admitted to participating in a scheme to increase the price of packaged bread from 2001 to 2015. According to court documents, Canada Bread, the largest bagged bread producer in the country, led with regular price increases and other producers like Weston followed, before getting retailers to agree on the price increase. Investigation is still ongoing at the time of writing, but it is likely that because the industry is highly concentrated, the largest players were able to fix prices with the explicit or tacit agreement of the few other dominant retailers such as Sobeys, Wal-Mart Canada, Metro and Giant Tiger. The near-monopoly position of these corporations guaranteed that competitors excluded from the agreement would not be able to undercut their price in a way that would hurt them. On the contrary, smaller players could well have followed suit and raised their prices to increase their own profits.[44]

As a final charting of trends since the early post-war years, consider the close relationship Brennan demonstrates between corporate concentration and the increasing internationalization of capital. He notes that the vast majority of global foreign direct investment (major cross-border investment in corporations) involves takeovers of existing firms, which is otherwise known as the transnational centralization of capital. Plotting the total amount of foreign direct investment coming into and going out of Canada, as a proportion of Canadian GDP, gives a sense of how internationalized Canadian capitalism is becoming. This statistic expresses how much investment capital is flowing into and out of Canada, relative to the size of the Canadian economy. In Figure 2.4, we see that until the 1990s the extent of internationalization kept pace with growth of the Canadian economy, hovering between two and three percent of GDP. But with the shift into continental and transnational "free trade," internationalization dramatically outpaced the growth of GDP. By the first decade of the twenty-first century, internationalization reached eight percent. Comparing this trend to the trend toward concentration of corporate share equity within the TSX 60, Brennan found that both evolved in close correspondence over six decades (as indicated by the high correlation coefficient). In the era of neoliberal globalization, increased internationalization of capital and increasing concentration of capital in the largest corporations have gone hand in hand. This is not a surprise. Recalling that most foreign direct investment involves takeovers of existing firms, these trends depict a close relationship between the concentration of capital within the largest firms and the transnational centralization of capital, a process in which the stock-exchange wolves swallow the lambs.[45] The result, as of the second decade of the twenty-first century, was a more internationalized Canadian economy in which corporate power had become concentrated in a few dozen companies.

Across the same decades, there was also a geographical concentration of corporate head offices in a few metropolitan command centres. In 1946, Montreal and Toronto were the only cities that really mattered for the corporate elite (and particularly for the financial sector). Of the top 103 corporations, 33 were headquartered in Montreal, and 31 were in Toronto. However, many industrial corporations had head offices and physical plants scattered outside the Toronto–Montreal axis in places such as Northern Ontario (six firms), Atlantic Canada (five firms) and

Winnipeg (four firms). Only one corporation was based in Calgary, while Vancouver was home to four. Half a century later, the spatial organization of corporate power had been simplified into a bipolar configuration. Of the top 103 corporations, Toronto hosted 38, Montreal 23 and two lesser centres in the west — Calgary and Vancouver — claimed 17 and 12, respectively. Outlying areas were rarely involved, and Toronto had decisively eclipsed Montreal as the country's corporate metropolis. This shift meant the further centralization of capital in large, multi-divisional corporations. Local management was subordinated to extra-local corporate strategies issuing from head offices in these few major cities. Geographical centralization created a sharper distinction between, on the one hand, four big cities that serve as command centres for corporate capitalists and, on the other, the rest of the country, overlaid upon deepening inequities in wealth and income.[46]

Figure 2.4. Relationship between corporate concentration and internationalization of capital[47]

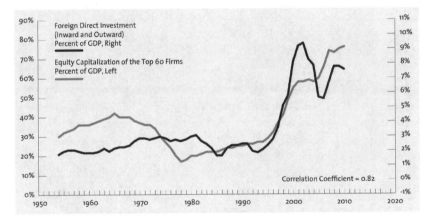

These developments also meant the ascent of the far west as a locus for corporate power. The geographical concentration of corporate power became simplified around four metropolitan centres in two quite distinct regions, which together housed 90 per cent of major corporations. Amid all these shifts, the one constant was the location of major financial institutions in the Montreal-Toronto area (with some internal shifting from the former to the latter). The rise of the west as a locale for the command of corporate capital was an industrial phenomenon (and, for Calgary, based almost entirely in the oil and gas sector). It did not disturb or displace the eastern-based financial sector.[48]

Chapter 3

CONTROLLING
THE CORPORATION

The Operational Power of Management

In this chapter (and the next three) we dig deeper into the architecture of corporate power — its social organization — and the specific modalities through which it is exercised. We rely in part on a power-structure analysis that maps the networks of individuals, corporations and key political and civic organizations as vectors of power and influence in and beyond the corporate economy. In view of the urgency of climate politics and the weight of the fossil fuel sector in Canada, much of our analysis features this industry and its interdependencies with sectors such as finance and media. As we will explain, the main centres of corporate power are economic, cultural and political.

In Chapter 2 we saw that it was not until the twentieth century that corporate power was fully consolidated in Canada and other advanced capitalist countries. Increasingly, this power has been projected beyond national states in the form of transnational corporations (TNCs) and banks, a global capital market and a complex of quasi-state institutions such as the World Bank and the World Trade Organization. In a globalizing world, corporations have the *structural power* to play one national workforce off against another. Union leaders and social activists worry about the prospect of a "race to the bottom," as workers in different countries undercut each other, and as TNCs search the planet for countries offering low wages, tax breaks and poor environmental standards, all to the ultimate benefit of transnational corporate capitalists.[1]

But how do we conceptualize corporate power in social terms? A good starting point is at the top: the corporate directorate. Having final authority over the corporation, the board of directors tops a hierarchy that reaches ultimately to the shop floor. Directorates are *sites* of authority within corporate power structures, and directors are *agents* of corporate power. Also, through the cross-appointment of directors, the boards of major corporations overlap with each other. Such interlocks draw directorates into an inter-corporate network, while also drawing directors into a socially integrated corporate elite.

Corporate power is Janus-faced. Its two faces are the economic and the cultural-political. Ultimately, it is rooted in the economy: the market system of commodity production, distribution and sales, as giant corporations and massive pools of capital concentrate social power in the capitalist class's top tier. In these circumstances, workers, communities and states must rely on the investments of capitalists for survival. We can distinguish three modalities of corporate economic power:

- *Operational* power means control of the labour processes within firms that produce and distribute commodities. It is the power of management, operating through a chain of command in which the scope of decision-making is narrowed as we move from top management to shop floor. Within large corporations, operational power takes a pyramidal shape. At the top is the chief executive officer, who reports directly to (and typically sits on) the board of directors. At the bottom are thousands of workers producing goods and services in workplaces that may be arrayed along commodity chains, across regions and countries. Operational power also involves subcontracting the economic activity along those commodity chains, from sourcing raw materials to selling the finished product.
- *Strategic* power involves control of the corporation itself, often by owning the largest bloc of shares. This is the power to set business strategies for the company, or for a set of companies assembled under common control as an enterprise. This power is rooted in the non-democratic character of corporate capital. Directors are annually "elected," but by the shareholders only. Workers, communities and consumers are excluded from the election. Moreover, the election is not based on one vote per person, but on one vote per corporate share owned. In practice, corporations are controlled by the wealthy few who own large concentrations of corporate shares.

It has long been recognized that dispersal of corporate shares across many small investors leads not to "people's capitalism" but to a stronger concentration of strategic power in the hands of a few major shareholders, whose ownership of a small proportion of voting shares can be sufficient to give them control of the board of directors and of the capital invested by smaller shareholders.[2]

- *Allocative* power stems from the control of credit, the money-capital on which large corporations depend. This power is especially important in expanding or retooling operations, launching takeover bids or coping with cash squeezes during crises. Allocative power entails various agents. Debtors on the receiving end of power might include non-financial capitalists as well as governmental and non-governmental organizations. Prime among the wielders of allocative power are the suppliers of financing, such as banks.[3]

Within the accumulation process, each of these modalities of economic power has its characteristic agents and sites. Operational power is wielded by managers within corporate management structures, but also across space. It spans all production activities along the commodity chain, from resource extraction at one location, through processes of transport, processing and manufacturing, to final consumption. Strategic power can involve complex alignments of major shareholders. Although centred in the board of directors, where strategic decisions are made, it often cuts across individual companies through inter-corporate ownership and interlocking directorates. The situation is similar for allocative power, which accrues to agents and organizations controlling the financial assets that fund new investment. As sociologists Beth Mintz and Michael Schwartz point out, financial institutions' control of pools of money-capital gives them (and the bankers who manage them) allocative power over corporations in need of financing. Allocative power may be centred in the financial institutions, but it entails complex relationships between banks and the corporations they lend to (who are in debt to them). These relationships are often visible in the structure of interlocking directorates.[4]

Corporate boards of directors show traces of all three kinds of power. Much of the research on corporate power has involved mapping the relations through which the largest corporations are linked together at the level of governance, which has been termed "power structure analysis." Viewed from this angle, directorate interlocks, inter-corporate ownership and the like are traces of allocative, strategic and operational modalities of economic power that, taken together, constitute a structure of "finance capital": an integration of big industry and high finance. As we saw in Chapter 2, finance capital is integral to corporate capitalism. The integration of capital pulls the largest corporations together into configurations of strategic control, capital allocation and operational command. At the level of individuals, this integration appears as a financial-industrial elite, a set of well-connected corporate directors whose affiliations with both industrial and financial corporations empower them as agents of strategic and allocative power: in other words, as finance capitalists.[5]

OPERATIONAL POWER: FROM EXECUTIVE SUITE TO SHOP FLOOR

Every corporation has its "c-suite," the top management positions, each beginning with the letter "c", and typically clustered in a space in which they can meet as a top-tier management team. The c-suite — the chief executive officer (CEO), chief financial officer (CFO), chief operating officer (COO) and others — is the most visible face of operational power. Immediately below it are strata of executive vice-presidents, senior vice-presidents, vice-presidents, assistant vice-presidents, divisional managers, plant managers and so on, each exercising a decreasing modicum of discretion. Operational power connects the dots between c-suites and actual workplaces. It is the top-down power of management.

For example, at SNC-Lavalin, a Canadian TNC based in Montreal, top management in 2015 consisted of a dozen executives, hierarchically organized as shown in Figure 3.1. CEO Robert Card was the only executive on the board of directors. COO Neil Bruce commanded four operating divisions (Oil and Gas, Infrastructure, Mining and Metallurgy, Power), each with its top manager, who also exercised "regional stewardship" in one area of the world beyond the firm's North American core business (which Card subtended). Other executives headed functional departments, including finance, human resources and legal affairs. Lavalin's 50,000 employees were subject to this group's operational power, but in turn, senior management was subject to strategic directives from the board of directors.

What do bosses do? Harvard economist Steve Marglin posed this question in 1974. His historical analysis of the rise of the factory system led

Figure 3.1. SNC-Lavalin organizational chart, 2018[6]

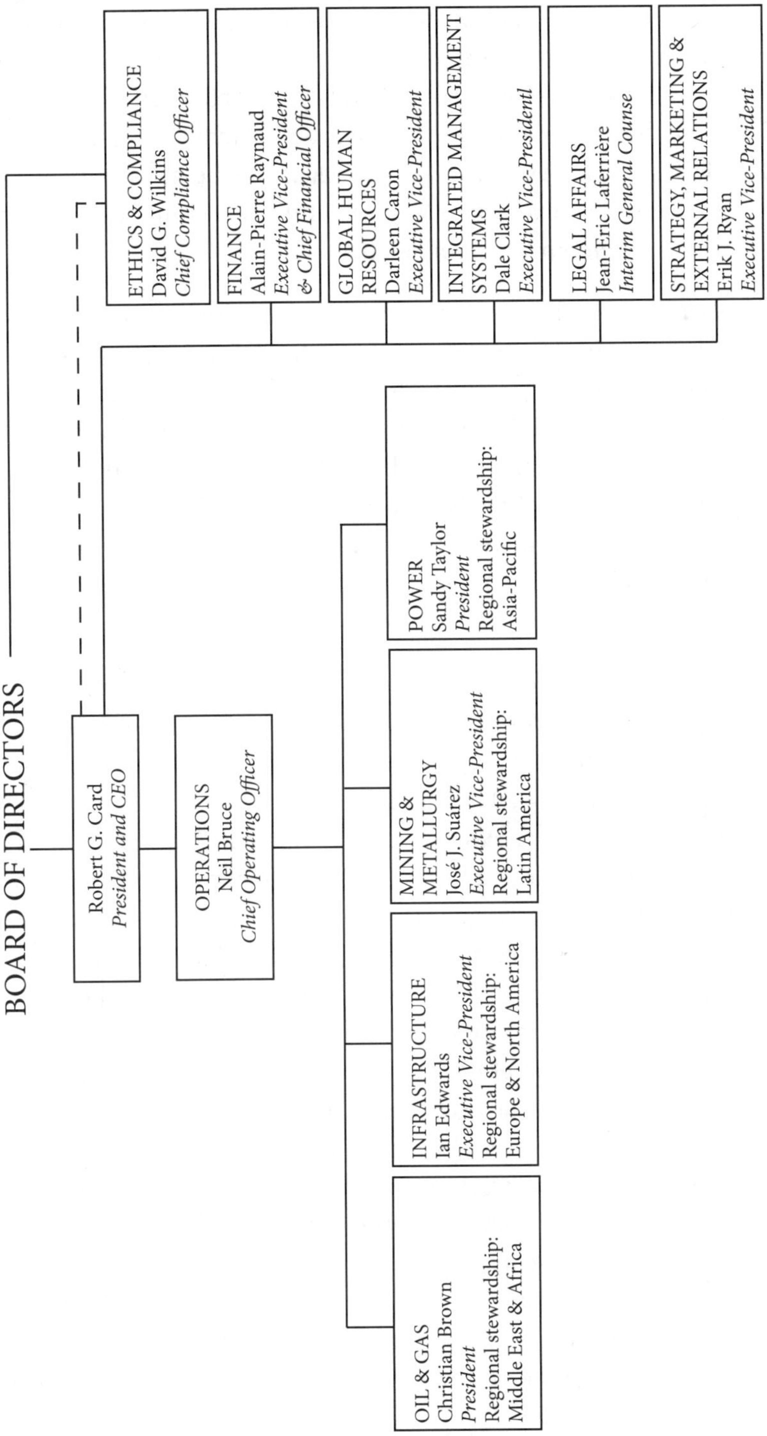

BOARD OF DIRECTORS

Robert G. Card
President and CEO

OPERATIONS
Neil Bruce
Chief Operating Officer

ETHICS & COMPLIANCE
David G. Wilkins
Chief Compliance Officer

FINANCE
Alain-Pierre Raynaud
Executive Vice-President & Chief Financial Officer

GLOBAL HUMAN RESOURCES
Darleen Caron
Executive Vice-President

INTEGRATED MANAGEMENT SYSTEMS
Dale Clark
Executive Vice-Presidentl

LEGAL AFFAIRS
Jean-Eric Laferrière
Interim General Counse

STRATEGY, MARKETING & EXTERNAL RELATIONS
Erik J. Ryan
Executive Vice-President

OIL & GAS
Christian Brown
President
Regional stewardship: Middle East & Africa

INFRASTRUCTURE
Ian Edwards
Executive Vice-President
Regional stewardship: Europe & North America

MINING & METALLURGY
José J. Suárez
Executive Vice-President
Regional stewardship: Latin America

POWER
Sandy Taylor
President
Regional stewardship: Asia-Pacific

him to conclude that the pyramidal structure of power within business enterprises is the result of class struggle reaching back into capitalism's formative era. In the struggle, capitalists learned that by centralizing production in factories they could directly discipline and supervise workers, and thereby appropriate more surplus. With the introduction of modern industry, factory workers were relegated to being "appendages" to its machinery. By the mid-nineteenth century, Marx and Engels could observe, in the *Communist Manifesto*, that

> Modern Industry has converted the little workshop of the patri-
> archal master into the great factory of the industrial capitalist.
> Masses of labourers, crowded into the factory, are organised like
> soldiers. As privates of the industrial army they are placed under
> the command of a perfect hierarchy of officers and sergeants. Not
> only are they slaves of the bourgeois class, and of the bourgeois
> State; they are daily and hourly enslaved by the machine, by the
> overlooker, and, above all, by the individual bourgeois manu-
> facturer himself.[7]

With the rise of corporations, the scale and complexity of labour processes grew. Large companies adopted multidivisional structures, with each division organized as a hierarchical pyramid, and with the emerging c-suite topping and coordinating all the divisions.

Many of today's corporate workplaces still resemble Marx and Engels's scenario of despotism, although much has been made of the "new economy" and, most recently, the "gig economy," which promises a "flexible" workplace where workers are empowered by multi-skilling and teamwork. Labour scholars Norene Pupo and Mark Thomas point out, however, that "the so-called new economy maintains many of the long-standing inequalities characteristic of capitalism." The "flexible" workplace "has increased employer control over work and heightened conditions of employment insecurity for workers." Rather than empowerment, "flexibility" is experienced as "work intensification due to lean production practices, and as insecure employment due to the proliferation of non-standard work arrangements."[8]

Of course, some workplaces are outright oppressive while others have a friendly vibe. But as Tom Malleson of Western University's Social Justice and Peace Studies Program states, "Every capitalist workplace has

Figure 3.2. Power-over, power-to, power-with

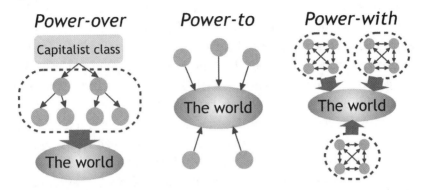

a governance structure that institutionalizes inequality, giving those at the top unaccountable power over those at the bottom." Indeed, operational power is fundamentally "power-over." At its core, operational power subjects subordinates to the domination and control of their activity, all to the benefit of those at the top. Although we often think of power in zero-sum terms — what I win you lose — in actuality power-over is simply one distinct form of power. As activists Lisa VeneKlasen and Valerie Miller suggest, "power-to" is the exercise of one's own agency in shaping one's world and one's self in it. "Power-with" develops as people gain collective strength through collaboration with peers, based on mutual support.[9]

Within corporations, power-over often masquerades as power-to and power-with, as in the notion that the "new economy" empowers workers through teamwork. Through such ideological frames, corporate management strives to persuade workers that the corporation's interest is aligned with their own. However, these alternative forms of power are important, and they do apply to certain workplaces. Power relations can be predominantly horizontal, as in collectives and cooperatives, which emphasize power-with and power-to. In a worker co-op, each worker owns a share, has a vote in decision-making, and gets a relatively equal part of net income. All three features support horizontal, egalitarian relationships and sharply contrast with the organization of property and power in corporations. We will reflect further on these alternatives to corporate power in this book's conclusion.

Capitalist workplaces, however, are organized through power-over. As Canadian sociologist James Rinehart observed in *The Tyranny of Work*, power-to (creative agency) is limited by the alienated character of work under corporate capitalism. As we saw above, the basic aim of production is private profit, not satisfaction of human needs. The productive apparatus is controlled by a relatively few individuals who operate it in their interests. This entails that "the majority of people, who will be obliged to work for the few, will be excluded from determining the products and process of labour." Rinehart shows how, in the early decades of the twentieth century, "scientific management" was used to reorganize workplaces by fragmenting complex tasks requiring skill, breaking them down into repetitive motions that could be performed by unskilled workers. "Taylorism," as it was called after its inventor Frederick Taylor, made the division of labour more complex and sharpened the division between manual and mental labour. As Taylor himself said, "All possible brain work should be removed from the shop and centred in the planning and laying-out department." The objective of all this was threefold. First, extreme division of tasks increased output for each unit of labour time, as each worker could perform repetitive tasks much faster. Second, it allowed greater managerial control over labour and reduced the level of skill required by much of the workforce. Third, it allowed corporations to hire less skilled workers who commanded lower wages. All these divisions functioned to break workers' control over their labour, appropriate their know-how into the new technologies and techniques of corporate capitalism and enhance capitalist profits.[10]

As the twentieth century played out, Taylorism was adapted and extended into white collar worlds, de-skilling clerical work in particular and increasing managerial control over it. As Graham Lowe has observed, "The ascendancy of corporate capitalism in Canada precipitated a revolution in the means of administration," with women predominantly recruited into "the new bottom layer of routine jobs produced by the administrative revolution." However, as work becomes emptied of creative experience, of power-to, workers tend to resist being treated like cogs in management's wheel. According to economist Richard Edwards, "The workplace becomes a battleground, as employers attempt to extract the maximum effort from workers and workers necessarily resist their bosses' impositions." Edwards has traced how this contested terrain was further reshaped as bureaucratic control became the predominant form of operational power. Simply put, corporations created elaborate rules and

procedures, including job descriptions, to govern the workplace imperson-
ally, through the rule of law. Workers were rewarded for following rules
and procedures and punished when they broke them. Closely identified
with the "managerial revolution" of the post-war era, bureaucratic control
remains the principal form of operational power today.[11]

Within the corporation, operational power is, as we suggested earlier,
multilayered, so that control over concrete decision-making is delegated
to lower ranks of management. The power that a corporate CEO wields
over the workplaces (s)he ultimately manages is mediated by layers of
management and subdivided, as with SNC-Lavalin, into various lines of
production, or in other words, into a complex bureaucracy. Transnational
business organization brings a further division between the top management of the parent firm and that of various subsidiaries in other countries.
For instance, in August 2017, SNC-Lavalin directly owned 75 subsidiaries
around the world, each with its own management taking direction from
the parent firm. Its larger subsidiaries had their own subsidiaries, extending operational power further down the chain. U.K.-based Kentz Corp.
Ltd., which Lavalin took over in 2014, had 14,000 employees and owned
(directly and indirectly) 82 firms in Africa, Europe, Asia, Australia and
the Americas. All told, Lavalin's direct and indirect subsidiaries numbered
312, giving its senior management mediated, operational power over vast
numbers of workers in many places of work.

Not indicated in the figure is the multitude of affiliates and independent
subcontractors to which a large part of the dirty business of production is
delegated. The latter, despite being nominally independent, must conform
to strict operational standards if the contracts with the TNC on which
they depend are to be renewed. Additionally, these more remote links
of the commodity chain are often located in jurisdictions where labour
and environmental laws are much more favourable to corporate profit. By
delegating large aspects of commodity production in this way, TNCs are
able to cut production costs and at the same time protect their corporate
image as their subcontractors take the blame for the poor working and
environmental conditions.

Political theorist Antonio Gramsci observed that the chain of command within a capitalist enterprise resembles that of the military. Middle
and lower layers of management can be compared to "subaltern officers
in the army." Having no autonomous initiative, their job is to execute the

Figure 3.3. SNC-Lavalin and its subsidiaries[12]

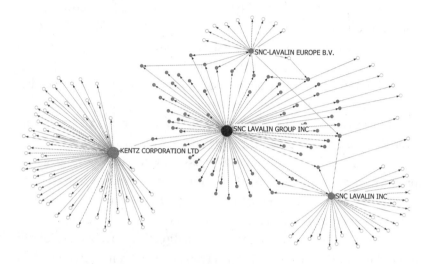

Key: The parent company is shown as the black circle in the middle, direct subsidiaries appear as dark gray circles, and indirect subsidiaries appear in light gray.
Arrows indicate the direction of ownership.

strategic plan that has been decided by those in control of the company.
Gramsci viewed such managers as the lower strata of organic intellectuals
(see Box 3.1). Their technical expertise is vital in enforcing the rule of
capital over the direct producers, within a complex division of labour.[13]

However, lower-level managers and supervisors are not themselves
capitalists. They are subject to operational power from above, even as
they wield it over their underlings. Like workers, they can be fired for not
fulfilling their assigned functions. And their salaries are a far cry from the
enormous sums that top executives claim (including valuable stock options
that give them a direct stake in the company). Economist Hugh Mackenzie
reports that in 2015 Canada's 100 highest-paid executives earned an average
of $9.5 million, or 193 times more than someone earning an average wage
($49,510). The disproportion is glaring. In contrast, lower-level manag-
ers occupy what sociologist Erik Olin Wright has called a "contradictory
class location," sandwiched between capitalism's two primary classes. They
play a crucial role, on capital's side, in enforcing bureaucratic rules and
procedures, yet their salaries place them closer to the upper layers of the
working class. Add to the picture the many relatively affluent professionals

BOX 3.1. ORGANIC INTELLECTUALS

Organic intellectuals, as described by Italian political theorist and activist Antonio Gramsci, articulate the interests of a class into a coherent set of ideas and proposals. Beyond producing analyses and narratives in support of one or another class project, they often also act as political organizers or as technicians who use their specialized skills to organize class-specific activities.

Many kinds of organic intellectuals serve to organize the interests of the capitalist class. In the strictly economic sphere, specialized technicians such as corporate managers, corporate lawyers and accountants provide the technical expertise needed in exercising operational power within corporations. Beyond the economic realm, multitudes of business journalists express the point of view of business in their publications. Academics working in business schools, economics departments and elsewhere convey pro-business ideas to each generation as it comes of age, and develop these ideas in their intellectual work. Retired politicians often join corporate boards of directors, dispensing advice on corporate strategy, while major corporations maintain small armies of lobbyists who advance their interests within the state. Hence, organic intellectuals play crucial roles in maintaining the system of corporate power, both by seeing to the everyday functioning of the capitalist economy and by extending the reach of capitalist influence in the political and cultural spheres.

Gramsci was also interested in the role intellectuals could play in constructing a counter-movement that could stand up to capitalist and corporate power by organizing workers as a class. In his role as the head of the Italian Communist Party, Gramsci himself epitomized that role. His influence still endures today.[14]

— engineers, designers, accountants that also participate in the corporation's complex division of labour and we have a veritable labyrinth, in which the basic class relation between capital and labour is blurred.[15]

Indeed, with the advent of bureaucratic control, capitalists gained a key ideological power in the workplace. Their physical presence disappeared while management-enforced rules and regulations came to govern individual workers. Richard Edwards puts it thus:

Figure 3.4. Compared earnings of workers and CEOS[16]

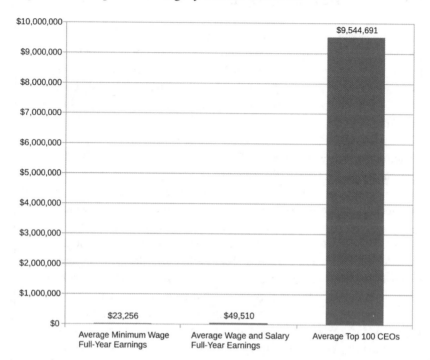

As workers were isolated from each other, and as the system was made distinct from the bosses who supervise it, the basic capitalist-worker relation tended to shrink from sight. The capitalist's power was effectively embedded in the firm's organization.

Operational power thus "connects the dots" between the concentrated corporate power at the top and the largely disempowered workforce at the bottom, in a way that obscures the former, under the cover of the corporate "rule of law."[17]

COMMODITY CHAINS AS CORRIDORS OF POWER

Corporate power, as operational power, also organizes the "commodity chains" that shape the landscape of contemporary Canada and the wider world. The entire global economy can be viewed as a vast assemblage of such chains. Each chain, as sociologist Jennifer Bair points out, consists of a "network of labour and production processes whose end result is a finished commodity." Commodity-chain analysis traces the trajectory of a product from its conception, through cultivation/extraction, processing, transport and final consumption, illuminating the various inter-organizational networks that cluster around a commodity.[18]

Like the chain of command within each corporation, commodity chains organize the actual operations of production and distribution, but they often involve multiple firms buying and selling each other's products. In fact, as capitalism has globalized, corporations have turned to subcontracting and outsourcing to reduce costs and maximize profit. This has changed the way transnational corporations are organized. In the earlier era of organized capitalism, the production process was vertically integrated and housed within the firm. Even today, the big, integrated fossil fuel corporations are organized to control the whole process of production, from extraction through refining, to distribution. Calgary-based Husky Energy, for instance, runs major conventional and tar sands oil and gas extraction operations in Western Canada; it owns refineries in Lloydminster, Alberta, Prince George, British Columbia, and Lima, Ohio; and it operates retail gas stations throughout Canada.

But in globalized production

> many, indeed most, of these activities are contracted out to other firms that specialize in one or another activity. The second firm becomes a supplier, subcontracted by the first and can also be subcontracted by other firms…. In this way, the old vertical hierarchy becomes a horizontal network.

The globalization of production has fragmented and decentralized production chains. Yet, as sociologist William Robinson writes, "This worldwide decentralization and fragmentation of the production process has taken place together with the *centralization* of command and control of the global economy in transnational [corporations]."[19]

Within commodity chains that often span continents, TNCs delegate operational power to the local firms, often in the Global South, with which they subcontract. The arrangement takes advantage of low wage rates and often lax regulations to generate enormous quantities of surplus value. These are then subdivided, as profit, between the local capitalists who directly exploit the workforce and the "lead firm" that technically purchases the product, within strict contractual terms that effectively bind the subcontractee to the subcontractor.

For example, Foxconn, a giant electronics manufacturer based in Taiwan, assembles parts of computers, phones and tablets for varied brands such as Apple, Microsoft, Sony, and Nokia in factories in mainland China. Harsh working conditions have been reported by workers, and the company is widely known for the 2010–11 wave of suicides among its employees. Yet subcontracting production in this way shields the reputation of U.S.- and European-based brands and thus protects profits that are distributed along the chain.[20] We are all familiar with other high-profile cases as Wal-Mart and Nike, which anti-sweatshop activism has named and shamed, resulting in at least cosmetic changes to the terms of their subcontractual arrangements. Although Nike founder Phillip Knight has often been praised for his business acumen, perhaps his genius as a capitalist was to figure out how to capture massive streams of surplus value from subcontractors without producing much of anything.[21]

Here, however, are three Canada-centred examples.

On April 24, 2013, Dhaka's eight-storey Rana Plaza collapsed, killing more than 1,100 workers. Investigative journalism revealed that some of Loblaw's Joe Fresh brand of clothes were manufactured in the Plaza. The killed and injured included employees of Loblaw's subcontractee, Bazlus Samad Adnan. It is not difficult to see why Loblaw would outsource from Bangladesh. At $38 per month, the country has the world's lowest minimum wage for garment workers. This tragedy shined a light on the transnational apparel commodity chain. Interviewed afterward, Adnan said Loblaws was his major client, bringing in approximately six million dollars each year, with a policy to "just ship it on time." A 15-year-old worker who survived the catastrophe (but whose mother perished) stated that she worked twelve hours a day, seven days a week, sewing pocket seams, and had worked in the industry for three years. Hers is one story behind the shiny labels that attract Canadian consumers to Joe Fresh and other brands.[22]

Ecologist and photographer Deborah Barndt has examined the commodity chain that brings the tomato from the Mexican fields to the Canadian table, "stopping along its trail at three key sectors that produce, commercialize, and sell the corporate tomato — agribusinesses, supermarkets, and fast-food restaurants." For corporations, the industry is enormously profitable, due in part to extremely low wages paid to workers in the Mexican fields, but also the relatively low wages of factory workers, supermarket cashiers and fast-food employees. But the profit also comes from what Jason Moore has dubbed capital's appropriation of "Cheap Nature," as in the low cost of land, carbon energy, water and other conditions of production. Cheap land, much of it previously cultivated by Indigenous Mexicans, becomes wasted by intensive agrochemical use, and Indigenous Mexicans are forced into wage labour in order to buy the food they previously grew. In turn, the low price of tomatoes and similar subsistence goods contributes to a lower cost to capital in reproducing Canada's working class.[23]

Barndt shows that the food production/consumption chain has become long and tangled, distancing consumers and workers alike from the actual fruit. This distancing keeps us in the dark as to the ecological, health-and-safety and social justice issues that are raised all along the chain, but it also alienates us from the web of life within which the tomato is produced. And it provides the capitalists at the top of the power structure with a ready alibi: "They can claim ignorance and innocence if something goes wrong, on down the line, with many aspects of production so far out of reach that they couldn't possibly know about it." Meanwhile, at each link in the chain, the operational power of corporate management organizes the labour process for maximal profit. As Barndt concludes:

> The architects and managers of global food production and consumption have standardized everything in the tomato chain: from the seeds hybridized and engineered for greater control, to the machinery, chemicals, and work practices in Mexico, from the skids and stickers that make border crossing quicker, to the supermarket designs and ready-made food, precut ingredients, and identical fast-food kitchens — all aimed at greater efficiency, higher yield, and greater profits.[24]

Our third example draws from our current research on corporate power in Canada's fossil fuel sector. Here, corporate power appears as control over energy networks: the production of the carbon-based energy that has literally powered capitalism since the industrial revolution. Through control over these networks, which are also commodity chains, corporate capital exercises a "thermodynamic" kind of power. According to economist Larry Elliott, it is this energy that drives nearly ninety percent of the global economy's vast machinery. How is corporate power wielded at ground level in the fossil fuel industry from carbon extraction and transport right through to final consumption?[25]

There are, of course, several kinds of fossil fuel — coal, natural gas, oil, bitumen — and for each, several ways of extracting carbon from the earth. Mountaintop removal — common in coal mining the U.S. Appalachians — is rare in Canada; bitumen mining now represents close to one-third of carbon resources produced in Canada (see Figure 3.5). And as the high quality, easily accessed deposits get tapped out, corporations turn to "extreme energy" that entails higher costs, greater ecological risk and often dirtier fossil fuel. This means fuel that emits far more pollution, including greenhouse gases, across the whole commodity chain, from extraction and refining to burning, producing a much more extreme impact on the climate and the land around extraction points and transport corridors. Bitumen from Canada's tar sands is an example of extreme energy, but so are oil from ultra-deep water wells off Newfoundland and fracked gas from Northeast BC.[26]

In contrast to the chain that links garment workers in Dhaka to shoppers in Toronto, or tomato-field workers in Mexico to fast-food diners in Halifax, Canada's carbon-extractive chain is staffed for the most part by high-wage workers, some of them unionized, using highly advanced technologies. Corporations are able to extract surplus value from these workers precisely due to the high productivity of their labour, which also means that these industries are among the most capital intensive. Rapid growth of this Alberta-centred industry since the 1960s meant that by 2010 Alberta had eclipsed Ontario as the province with the largest share of the nation's capital stock, claiming 30 percent of the total according to political economists Geoffrey McCormack and Thom Workman. Prompted by state-subsidized high profit rates, the national economy had shifted toward fossil fuels as the driver of industrial accumulation, leading former Prime Minister Stephen Harper to herald Canada's emergence as an "energy superpower."[27]

Yet all this massive investment and profit-taking actually generated relatively few jobs for workers. Political scientists Greg Albo and Lilian Yap point out that in Canada, total employment in fossil fuel extraction, coal and petroleum manufacturing and support activities is about 120,000,

Figure 3.5. Aerial view of Syncrude's Mildred Lake mining site

Photo credit: Alex McLean[28]

well less than 1 percent of Canada's workforce, with tar sands employment at around 20,000 workers (only a fraction of whom are engaged in extraction itself). Moreover, "if many of these jobs are well-paid, they are also surprisingly precarious and insecure as projects and output volumes wind up and down; and they have come to include a 'second-tier' of migrant workers with limited rights." Significantly, 23,000 Indigenous people live within Alberta's tar sands region. While some of them are employed in the industry or in industry-related activities, all of them are exposed to pollution of the land, air and wildlife by bitumen extraction. Indigenous sociologist Angele Alook and her colleagues note that

> when Indigenous people living in areas close to industry engage in their traditional lifestyles of living off the land, including consuming wildlife, they are at heightened exposure to pollutants in the ecosystem. However, these concerns don't seem to be taken seriously by oil corporations and the provincial and federal governments.[29]

From Alberta, oil and gas flow through an elaborate network of pipelines. They move from extraction sites to refineries in the U.S. and in Canadian cities such as Edmonton, Vancouver and Sarnia. Refined products (including fuels and plastics) are then transported to locations where they are consumed, either in other industrial processes or by retail consumers. Pipelines are massive, fixed-capital investments. They require extensive financing (and state subsidization through low taxes and royalties), and they only generate profit slowly, over their long life cycle.

For corporate capital, continued control over energy is just as crucial as the revenue generated from pipelines and other elements of fixed capital embedded in energy infrastructure. To maintain this control, economic power must be combined with "social license," a form of hegemonic power that identifies the corporate interest with the general interest. But as people have become more aware of the ecological risks surrounding fossil fuels, pipelines have become the weakest link in the carbon commodity chain. Corporate power as control over energy flows is highly contested, particularly at flashpoints along pipelines, where Indigenous, land-based resistance to continuing colonization often combines with environmental activism in attempting to block pipeline construction or repurposing.

Commodity-chain analysis situates and illuminates the flashpoints at which issues of corporate power, ecology and public health and safety may come into open contestation. Each link in a given commodity chain (from extraction to final sales and consumption) is a site of corporate power. At each of these sites, potential issues appear regarding economic equity, governance, regulation and public participation, ecological health and risk, land title and sovereignty. Although revenues dispensed to workers, landholders, and Indigenous communities may win support, the historical record is replete with examples of political contention at flashpoints. A noteworthy recent development is the Treaty Alliance Against New Pipeline Development. Signed in September 2016, the agreement commits over fifty First Nations and Tribes from Canada and the United States to collaborate to stop proposed oil sands pipeline, tanker and rail projects on their lands and waters.[30]

Whether it is exercised within chains of command or across commodity chains, operational power is the most concrete modality of corporate power. It directly structures the workplaces, labour processes, landscapes and ecologies of corporate capitalism, enabling large corporations to

Figure 3.6. Existing and planned pipelines to the United States[31]

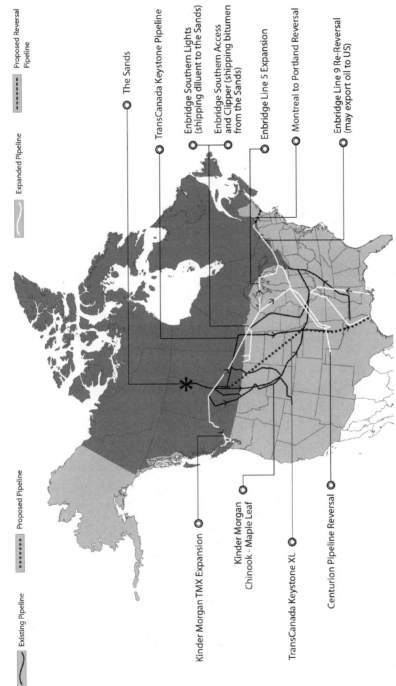

Proposed Reversal Pipeline

Expanded Pipeline

Proposed Pipeline

Existing Pipeline

The Sands

TransCanada Keystone Pipeline

Enbridge Southern Lights (shipping diluent to the Sands)

Enbridge Southern Access and Clipper (shipping bitumen from the Sands)

Enbridge Line 5 Expansion

Montreal to Portland Reversal

Enbridge Line 9 Re-Reversal (may export oil to US)

Kinder Morgan TMX Expansion

Kinder Morgan Chinook - Maple Leaf

TransCanada Keystone XL

Centurion Pipeline Reversal

appropriate the economic surplus that fuels profits. There are, however, forms of economic power that are detached from these operational details of production and distribution. An important one is the slippery reality of finance capital.

Chapter 4

CONTROLLING THE CAPITALIST ECONOMY

Strategic Power and Capital Allocation

If the operational power of management traces the path of capitalist domination from c-suite to shop floor and along commodity chains, it does not identify who controls the corporation itself. As one of us has surmised, "the strategic power to direct the corporations that dominate advanced capitalism is highly centralized in three identifiable kinds of agents: major shareholders, top-level salaried managers, and financiers." Sociologist John Scott notes further that these three categories do not necessarily refer to separate individuals: "The financiers who provide loan capital, for example, may also be large shareholders, and major shareholders may be members of the executive hierarchy." All three agents may be represented on the corporation's board of directors. The board thus brings together the top tier of operational management (in the CEO), the major shareholders and the major financiers or creditors (who are often directors of financial institutions that have lent to the firm). In this chapter we focus on the power wielded by major shareholders and creditors.[1]

POWER AS STRATEGIC CONTROL

Let's begin with the shareholders and the modality of power we call strategic control.

As we emphasized in Chapter 2, the corporate form — the parcelling of ownership into many tradeable shares offering limited liability to investors — is integral to corporate power. By amassing a strategic bloc of shares — say, 10 percent or more — an investor can (if the rest of the share capital is scattered among many small investors) control a corporation whose capital is many times greater than the value of the shares held. This further concentrates corporate power in the hands of people and corporations that assemble such strategic blocs. Strategic control refers to the ability to control the composition of the board of directors, based on ownership of such strategic blocs. Of course, the vast majority of corporations in Canada are not listed on stock exchanges. Their shares are not publicly traded, but are "closely held" by one capitalist or possibly a few associated investors, who wield absolute strategic power over the corporations they own outright.

In Canada, beginning with John Porter's research based on data from 1960, studies have consistently shown that most publicly traded corporations are controlled by individuals, families and other corporations. Very few are "widely held," without identifiable controlling interests. This means that the so-called "managerial revolution" — the dispersal of corporate shares resulting in the control of corporations by professional managers — is a myth. At the time of writing, the most recently published comprehensive study of corporate ownership and control in Canada confirmed that, among 1,120 Canadian-controlled corporations whose shares are publicly listed on stock exchanges, 56.17 percent are ultimately controlled by wealthy families, and only 17.79 percent are without a clearly identifiable controlling interest. Pyramidal shareholding (discussed below) contributes to the concentration of ownership, enabling ultimate owners to control giant corporations by holding a relatively small bloc of share capital.[2]

Typically, a company controlled by a single family will have a small directorate composed of family members and trusted assistants. This especially applies to the vast majority of corporations, which are privately owned, usually by single families. But what of the relatively few though important cases (199 of the 1,120 just mentioned) where no one owning interest is in a position to dominate? As John Scott has documented, a company lacking any one dominant shareholder will typically have a more complex constellation of interests represented on the board. This broad group of stakeholders may include various financial institutions and institutional investors whose combined ownership would be large enough to give them minority control (greater than 10 percent of shares), but they lack the unity required to wield control in an active way. This form of strategic control is virtually invisible, unless internal corporate management fails to deliver on profit, or an external capitalist makes a hostile takeover bid. In the former case, the controlling constellation might initiate a change in top management. In the latter, owners might mobilize their combined share bloc against the unwanted suitor to protect their collective investment.[3]

In these scenarios, institutional investors such as the Canada Pension Plan (CPP), the Ontario Teachers' Pension Plan or Québec's Caisse de dépôt et placement often play key roles. These are corporations that manage pension funds and other pools of financial capital. Before the 1990s, when Canadian (and global) capitalism became sharply more financialized, pensions were recognized by all as deferred wages, as income to workers placed in trust to be paid out, with interest, after retirement. This is how the CPP operated, for instance. As an aspect of neoliberal policy, deregulation of these funds enabled their managers to pursue higher rates of profit by investing in corporate shares. In 2005, the CPP was allowed to redeploy investments from Canadian corporate shares to foreign assets. As of March 13, 2017, the CPP Investment Board held shares in 150 Canadian companies (worth a total of $13 billion) and in 2,908 foreign companies (worth $110 billion). Its corporate shareholdings reflect a very high degree of transnationalization, with investments in more than 150 Chinese companies, for example.[4]

Recent years have seen pension funds redefined. No longer viewed as workers' deferred wages, they are now seen simply as another form of investing in corporations, mainly very large ones. As they have accumulated this capital, institutional investors have become important players within constellations of interest. They rarely take dominant ownership positions in corporations, but often are in a position of influence, along with other members of a constellation. By 2015, it was reported that the assets of Canada's ten largest pension funds had topped $1 trillion. That compares to a total gross domestic product of $1.986 trillion.[5]

Investment companies, in contrast to constellations of interest, often do take controlling positions in the corporations they buy into. Power Corporation of Canada is a good example. A family-owned corporation, it has played an important role in Canadian finance capital since it formed in 1925. From the 1970s, under the direction of the Desmarais family,

Power Corp shifted its capital from the energy and electric utility sectors into a bevy of financial institutions. Concurrently, Power internationalized its holdings to include major stakes in European corporations, through Groupe Bruxelles Lambert (GBL), an investment company it controls in collaboration with the Frère family of Belgium.[6]

It is share ownership blocs that enable the Desmarais to control a vast empire of corporations in Canada, Europe and other countries. This empire is directed by the two sons of its founder, Paul Desmarais: Paul Jr. and André. The value of their personal fortune is approximately $8.4 billion, placing them seventh among Canada's billionaires, according to *Canadian Business* magazine's 2018 ranking of Canada's 100 richest people and families. Most of that personal fortune is invested in Power's share capital.

The Desmarais family owns a little more than half of Power's shares, guaranteeing uncontestable control of the corporation. At the time of writing, Power Corporation's market value to investors — its market capitalization — is $12.65 billion, all of which is under the family's strategic control. But through the pyramiding of inter-corporate ownership, they actually control assets that, according to the company website, were worth $435 billion as of June 30, 2017. Much of this capital is controlled through Power Financial Corporation. Power Corporation owns 65.6 percent of that financial conglomerate, and in turn Power Financial has majority control of a host of Canadian financial institutions. The Power Corporation website informs us that Power Financial's assets under administration (mostly held by those financial institutions) total $1.408 trillion, up from $181 billion in 2001.[7]

On the other side of the Atlantic Ocean, Power Financial's 50 percent ownership of Parjointco gives it control of majority-owned Pargesa, which owns half of the shares of Groupe Bruxelle Lambert (GBL), an investment company that holds strategic blocs in a number of major European corporations such as German sportswear manufacturer Adidas and French distiller Pernod Ricard. As mentioned, the Frère family owns the other half of GBL. Through GBL, the allied families own 9.4 percent of LafargeHolcim, the world's largest cement and construction manufacturing company. LafargeHolcim's 852 subsidiaries in 80 countries include Lafarge Canada, which has long been the dominant firm in this sector of the Canadian economy. The Canadian subsidiary is the result of a merger of Lafarge

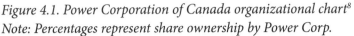

Figure 4.1. Power Corporation of Canada organizational chart[8]
Note: Percentages represent share ownership by Power Corp.

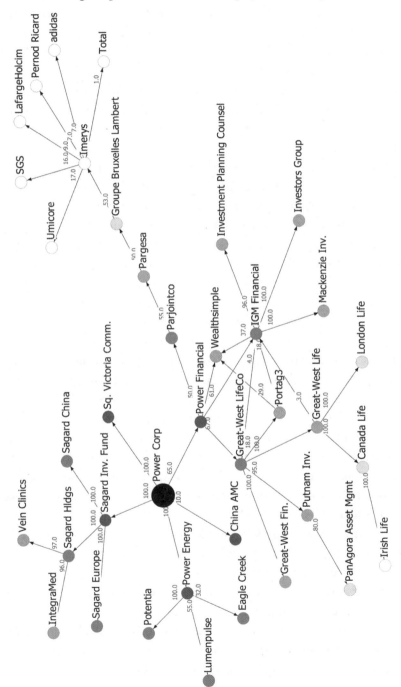

Canada and Holcim Canada, which occurred simultaneously with the 2015 merger of their European parents to form LafargeHolcim, further centralizing capital in this industry in Europe, Canada and across the globe. Swiss billionaire Thomas Schmidheiny, who inherited Holcim from his father, retains an 11.4 percent stake in LafargeHolcim and is the largest single shareholder. He also sits on the company's twelve-member board of directors, along with Dieter Spälti (who has administered Schmidheiny's investments since 2002) and interim CEO Beat Hess. But the Desmarais/Frère interests are also directly represented on the LafargeHolcim board, through Paul Desmarais Jr. (Chairman and Co-CEO of Power Corporation and Vice-Chair of GBL) and Gérard Lamarche (Co-CEO of GBL).

The example of LafargeHolcim takes us outside the realm of Canadian capitalism, but it shows how major capitalists based in Canada control corporate assets on a transnational basis. More than that, we see on the board a constellation of interests made up of dominant shareholders as well as the CEO. Finally, this example shows how, through pyramiding of share ownership, a family like the Desmarais can hold a major strategic stake in a giant TNC on the basis of a comparatively small investment, enabling finance capitalists, in effect, to control "other people's money." At the time of writing, LafargeHolcim's market capitalization is $46.5 billion Canadian. Power Corporation's capital passes through four companies before it reaches LafargeHolcim and is effectively diluted at each step while strategic control is maintained. Following the chain of ownership, the LafargeHolcim stake ties up 0.856 percent of Power's entire capital, a tiny fraction. This means that approximately $57.3 million of the Desmaraises' $6.7 billion buys them collaborative control, in a constellation of interests, of a Swiss TNC whose value to investors is nearly one thousand times greater than the small slice of the family fortune that enables this strategic control.[9]

The entire set of firms in the Desmarais/Frères orbit, numbering in the thousands if one includes subsidiaries and affiliates, comprises a financial group, not unlike the group led by Donald Smith at the inception of Canadian corporate capitalism, though far more internationalized. But besides strategic holdings that bring with them corporate directorships, Power Corporation participates in the wider constellations of interest at the heart of Canadian finance capital. The most important of these converge on Canada's leading banks, which own each other, to a considerable

Figure 4.2. Cross-ownership among the largest Canadian banks and financial institutions[10]

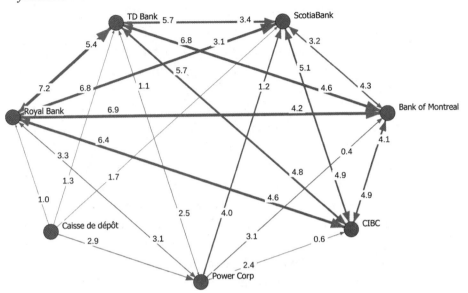

degree. Figure 4.2 illustrates the network of inter-corporate ownership among the five biggest Canadian banks plus Power Corporation and the Caisse de dépôt.

The thickness of each line is proportionate to the size of the inter-corporate ownership between a pair of firms. The links that make up this network are "directed lines." To show how much of one firm's shares another firm owns, we have varied the size of the arrowheads and labelled the lines with the actual percentage of shares owned. For instance, The Royal Bank of Canada owns 6.8 percent of the Bank of Nova Scotia (ScotiaBank), but the Bank of Nova Scotia owns only 3.1 percent of the Royal Bank of Canada. Except for the Caisse, which is wholly owned by the government of Quebec, each of the seven is substantially owned by the others, as a group. Nearly 10 percent of Power Corporation is owned by the other six, with the Royal Bank of Canada claiming 3.3 percent of outstanding shares and the Caisse claiming 2.9 percent. Between 20 and 25 percent of the shares of each bank are held by this very select group of financial centres. Among the banks, the Royal is the most extensively invested in its fellow banks (which, we should remember, are supposedly its competitors), averaging 5.1 percent ownership of the other four. The

Bank of Nova Scotia is the least invested, averaging 3.7 percent owner-ship of the other four, which compares to Power Corporation's average ownership stakes in the five big banks (3.02 percent).

Banks are prohibited by law from sharing directors, but one can see in this tight network of inter-corporate ownership that they collectively own each other. This offers them effective immunity from possible hostile takeovers, and, through their cross-ownership, binds them into a common role that Karl Marx once called "general managers" of financial capital. Power Corporation and the Caisse are also immune from takeover due to their majority ownership by a family (Power) and the state (Caisse).

These major centres of financial capital are, of course, heavily invested not only in each other, but also in a wide range of other economic sectors. The concept of finance capital, which we introduced in Chapter 2 (see Box 2.1), is helpful on this point. Under corporate capitalism, there is a close co-dependency between financial and industrial capital. Corporate empires such as the Desmarais' exemplify this symbiosis, particularly as it is achieved through amassing blocs of corporate shares (a form of financial capital) that affords strategic control over various industrial and other corporations. We can see the same integration of capital if we focus on individual industrial firms.

Calgary-based TransCanada Corp is one of the major industrial com-panies whose capital has gravitated to Alberta's tar sands. Founded in 1951 to supply natural gas to Eastern Canada, TransCanada internation-alized its investments in the 1980s with pipeline projects in Indonesia, Chile and Malaysia, but later it refocused its business strategy on Canada and the U.S. By acquiring several companies in the past three decades it has become one of the largest energy infrastructure firms in North America. TransCanada entered the oil pipeline business in 2010, with completion of phase one of the Keystone Pipeline, pumping oil from Alberta to a refinery in Illinois. Several extensions followed. Originally a partnership with ConocoPhillips, TransCanada bought ConocoPhillips's Keystone stake in 2009. The Keystone XL extension, originally slated for completion in December 2012, became a major flashpoint as environ-mentalists, local landowners and Indigenous communities mobilized in opposition. Although legislation to approve Keystone XL was passed by the U.S. Congress, President Barack Obama used his veto to block the process. Obama noted that the pipeline would create a miniscule number of long-term jobs and would undercut the U.S.'s "global leadership" on climate change. In January 2017, four days into his presidency, Donald Trump signed a permit to allow the pipeline to be built.[11]

As of 2016, TransCanada's major shareholder is U.S.-based Columbia Pipeline Group. However, in a $13 billion purchase, TransCanada took over Columbia in July 2016. In effect, TransCanada is its own major shareholder, again protecting it from possible takeover by another capitalist interest. There are twelve other key shareholders of TransCanada.[12]

Table 4.1. TransCanada Corporation's main external shareholders[13]

Shareholding corporation	Percent held	Country of domicile	Type of firm
Royal Bank of Canada	7.08	Canada	Bank
Toronto-Dominion Bank	4.19	Canada	Bank
Power Corporation of Canada	3.86	Canada	Investment
Bank of Montreal	3.70	Canada	Bank
Bank of Nova Scotia	3.32	Canada	Bank
Deutsche Bank AG	2.83	Germany	Bank
Canadian Imperial Bank of Commerce	2.59	Canada	Bank
Wellington Management Group LLP	2.53	U.S.	Asset management
Vanguard Group Inc	2.43	U.S.	Asset management
fmr llc	2.00	U.S.	Asset management
Capital Group Co Inc	1.97	U.S.	Asset management
Caisse de dépôt et placement du Québec	1.75	Canada	Pension fund

As of August 2017, TransCanada's top twelve external shareholders were mostly institutional investors.[14] All twelve manage vast pools of financial capital. They include all five big Canadian banks, plus Germany's largest bank (Deutsche Bank), an investment company, a pension fund and four asset managers. The latter administer a variety of investment funds, including pensions, and do not aspire to strategic control but rather seek to optimize profit by buying and selling shares in many companies. We can see that strategic control resides firmly in Canada. Not counting TransCanada's self-ownership, the domestic constellation of interests includes Canada's biggest banks, its biggest investment company and its biggest pension fund. It holds 26.49 percent of share capital and thus the same percentage of votes at TransCanada's annual general meeting. But foreign investors also claim slices of the pie (and a steady stream of profit). Deutsche Bank owns nearly three percent while four leading U.S.-based asset managers each claim about two percent.

In these examples of strategic control, we see how extensively corporate capital has become "socialized" as finance capital among the leading agencies of the capitalist class and how concentrated power is within a few such centres. These centres are both corporations and individuals. The Desmarais family, finance capitalists who control Power Corporation, wields enormous power that transects national borders. But so do the CEOs of Canada's banks and of TransCanada Corporation. Although these chief executives do not own massive share blocs, they are at the top of the hierarchy of operational power and they participate in strategic decision-making on the corporate directorate. Also, the common practice of rewarding top managers with stock options and other profit-based incentives that dwarf the size of their salaries gives them a compelling interest in maximizing corporate profitability. For instance, TransCanada CEO Russ Girling's base salary in 2016 was $1.3 million. However, as additional rewards, he received $2.21 million in "short-term incentive," $3 million in "Executive Share Units" and an additional $3 million in TransCanada stock options. These brought his compensation package to $9.51 million, a 12 percent gain on the previous year. However, that compensation does not include the dividends Girling would have received from the bloc of TransCanada shares he has accumulated through stock options since he became CEO in 2010, which were valued at $12.57 million.[15]

Looking at TransCanada's board of directors and their other corporate affiliations gives a view of the web of relationships in which the company is embedded and on which directors can draw to orient the company's activities. Out of TransCanada's twenty-nine directors and executives, twelve participate in the governance of other large corporations. For example:

Figure 4.3. TransCanada's board interlocks[16]

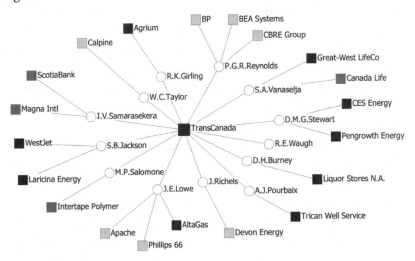

- CEO Russ Girling serves as a director of Calgary-based agro-chemical firm Agrium.
- Independent director John E. Lowe helps steer three other energy-sector firms in Canada and the U.S.
- Paula Reynolds sits on the board for oil and gas giant BP and arms manufacturer BEA Systems, both based in the U.K., as well as on CBRE, a very large real estate firm based in California.
- Indira Samarasekera, past president of the University of Alberta (2005–2015), links TransCanada to the financial and manufacturing sectors through the boards of ScotiaBank and auto parts maker Magna International.

In all, TransCanada's social circle extends to eight different sectors and reaches to all regions of Canada as well as the U.S. and the U.K. As sociologist Michael Useem explains, such a web of directorship interlocks gives access to a broad range of information on the ups and downs of various sectors on which the board can rely for strategic planning.[17]

THE ALLOCATIVE POWER OF FINANCE

Allocative power is wielded by financial corporations through their control of vast pools of money-capital. Those in need of financing, whether they are corporations, states or other agencies, are at the mercy of these institutions. As Michael Schwartz and Beth Mintz observe in their study, *The Power Structure of American Business*, "The choices made by financials to support one firm or industry — or even a country — over another, or to enter or depart from one area of investment, often represent the crucial, determining reality within which nonfinancial corporations operate." The highly concentrated state of Canada's financial sector means an intense concentration of allocative power. In 2015, the big five banks accounted for 82.25 percent of banking industry assets.[18]

Allocative power is distinct from strategic control, although both are based in ownership of financial capital. As Athar Hussein clarified some years ago, the sale of shares by a corporation is actually a form of borrowing, but the borrower never repays the principal (although corporations sometimes "buy back" the shares they have issued). Typically, the shares circulate on stock markets, paying out dividends — a portion of profit — to their owners. These shares fluctuate in value according to investors' judgements of their future profitability, and investors in turn buy and sell them to make profits. In the past few decades, there has been an explosion in the volume and kinds of tradeable "financial assets," from traditional shares and bonds to derivatives of various kinds. Derivatives are the purest form of what Marx called "fictitious capital," as they lack any connection whatsoever to the world of production from which surplus value issues. They are purely speculative paper assets, as Wall Street expert Doug Henwood explains:

> Essentially, derivatives involve the exchange of money and promises; nothing as semi-substantial as a stock or bond is involved. For example, a Swiss bank with an asset denominated in yen might swap it for a dollar-denominated one held by a British bank. Or a bank with a floating (adjustable) rate asset can swap it for a fixed-rate asset. More precisely, the parties exchange the payment streams associated with each asset (interest, for example, not the underlying loan or bond) — that is, each agrees to make specified payments on specified dates. If that sounds incomprehensible, that's OK; many senior bank execs and regulators don't fully understand either.

Globally, it is estimated that "98% of the value of monetary transactions in the world are speculative, only 2% involve actual use-values." Only corporate shares confer ownership rights, and the potential for a capitalist to control a firm individually or as part of a constellation of interests, which is why we have highlighted their strategic role in the structure of corporate power. Yet other kinds of securities, as well as loans, make up a large percentage of financial capital, and lenders have first call on a company's assets in cases of bankruptcy.[19]

Sometimes, this priority comes as a rude awakening to workers. In October 2017, the bankrupt Sears Canada announced that the pensions of its 16,921 current and retired employees would be allocated to Sears's creditors, leaving the workers with precious little in their retirement. Although Sears underfunded its pension plan for nearly a decade before filing for bankruptcy in 2017, it also paid out nearly 3 billion dollars in special dividends to shareholders between 2005 and 2013. To add further insult, the company also sought and received court approval to dole out $6.5 million in bonuses to its executives as the company was being liquidated.[20]

Allocative power shapes the entire economy and society, which is why Mintz and Schwartz viewed the major financial institutions as centres of "financial hegemony." In a globalizing world, this power is wielded transnationally as well as within national societies, and it applies to states as well as corporations. As a key source of the capitalist class' increasing "structural power," political scientists Stephen Gill and David Law point to the enhanced international capital mobility that comes with the transnationalization of investment and the consolidation of international financial markets on which securities trade. In these circumstances, corporations and states in need of funds must maintain business confidence or risk losing access to those funds. If a government brings in pro-labour policies, or a corporation makes investments that appear to stray from maximal profitability, financial capitalists can respond, instantaneously, with an "investment strike." When workers strike, they withdraw their labour-power. When capitalists strike, they withdraw their capital. For a country, such a strike means massive divestment, as funds flow to more promising places, provoking a collapse in the value of the currency. Particularly for open economies like Canada's, a collapsing currency raises the specter of inflation as the cost of imports skyrockets. Hence, the international mobility of financial capital "can swiftly force governments that deviate from policies seen as suitable by 'the market,' to change course." In our era of neoliberal globalization, this structural power is a crucial political lever, a means of disciplining governments that stray from the neoliberal agenda and "under-performing" corporations. The banks that lend money-capital to large corporations and to states thus wield a structural power, allocating funds to what they deem the most promising prospects in terms of their profitability, and diverting them from other ventures with lower expected returns. In the process, they shape the landscape of corporate capitalism, according to the logic of profit maximization.[21]

Consider one example, prompted by a speech Royal Bank of Canada (RBC) CEO David McKay gave to the Edmonton Chamber of Commerce in September 2016. McKay urged the federal government to help get fossil fuel resources to market by approving new pipelines and other energy infrastructure. Doing so, he claimed, was crucial to the transition to a "cleaner economy." McKay's plea was enthusiastically re-tweeted the following day by Canada's Minister of Environment, Catherine McKenna. Logicians would have fun with the idea that ramping up fossil fuel production and building new pipelines will help Canada achieve its stated goals on the climate change front. But McKay tipped his hand as to what is at stake for RBC when he described the bank as "Canada's leading bank, for conventional, non-conventional and renewable resources." Indeed, RBC, which is Canada's biggest bank, has an intimate relationship with carbon-based capital and a direct interest in its continued accumulation.[22]

On the capital allocation side, RBC had $7 billion tied up in loans to the oil and gas sector, accounting for 4.6 percent of its total business loans, in 2016. Like other banks, RBC allocates capital selectively to the entire range of industries, so the credit it supplies to the carbon-extractive sector is just a piece of the action. However, our investigation revealed that more than half of RBC's business loans that are not being repaid or at risk of default were, at the time, in the oil and gas sector, reflecting continuing challenges in the wake of the 2014 crash in oil prices. For RBC, it is important that its loans be redeemed, and that means cranking up the machinery of carbon extraction, not winding it down.[23]

Banks do not reveal details on business loans, but we know from reports on inter-corporate ownership that RBC owns pieces of all twelve of the largest Canadian carbon-extractive corporations whose shares are publicly traded. In addition to its stake in TransCanada Corporation (shown above), this includes 7.9 percent ownership of Enbridge Inc, 7.6

percent of Pembina Pipeline Corp., 6.4 percent of Gibson Energy Inc., 6.1 percent of Cenovus, 4.0 percent of Suncor Energy Inc. and 1.9 percent of Imperial Oil Ltd.[24]

RBC's intimate relationship with Canada's fossil fuel sector is also evident at the level of corporate governance. Five of RBC's directors and top executives sit on the boards of eight corporations in that sector, two of which number among the twelve biggest (Imperial Oil and Suncor). To say the least, RBC is not a neutral observer of energy and climate policy. Its CEO's call for more pipelines, as part of a green energy transition, was simply a defence of carbon-capital interests, which are also RBC interests. This case study shows that financial institutions like RBC, as powerful capital allocators and owners, are also enablers of fossil capital. If we are concerned about the role of corporate power in driving forward one of the most dangerous forces of our time — human-induced climate change — our analysis must take in these enablers.[25]

Figure 4.4. The Royal Bank of Canada's leadership interlocks with eight Canadian fossil-fuel companies[26]

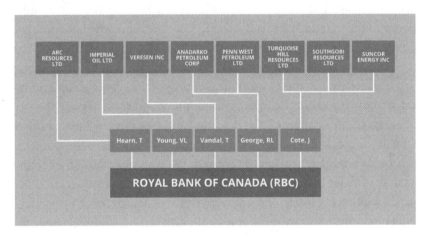

Chapter 5

THE CORPORATE ELITE
A Tangled Web of Oligarchic Power

Corporate power, as power-over, is centred in a corporate elite. The elite is composed of the directors and top executives of the largest corporations, held together through their interlocking directorships and other shared affiliations in private clubs and the like. The most descriptive way of characterizing the corporate elite is to consider simply the set of individuals occupying positions of economic authority. In *The Vertical Mosaic*, John Porter found that the key members of the elite are those who hold multiple directorships in the largest corporations. Such interlocking directors "are the ultimate decision makers and coordinators within the private sector of the economy. It is they who at the frontiers of the economic and political systems represent the interest of corporate power. They are the real planners of the economy." The directors and executives whose multiple affiliations create interlocking directorates are also at the centre of what can be termed the "corporate community." American power-structure analyst William Domhoff defines the corporate community as "all those profit-seeking organizations connected into a single network by overlapping directors."[1] Our own interpretation is that the corporate elite is the "leading edge" of a capitalist class whose other members also include the owners and top executives of mid-sized and smaller companies.

The concept of a corporate elite comprises all three of these notions: top authority positions, cohesive community and leading edge. The idea of a leading edge is particularly illuminating as it highlights the elite's significance as a condensation of capitalist class power, based in the strategic, allocative and operational modalities we analyzed in the previous two chapters. Yet corporate power is more than the sum of these three parts. This is where an analysis of the corporate elite, as a whole, is important. All three modalities of economic power are active in shaping the network. Its composition and structure change with the rise and decline of specific industries, realignments of financial groups, corporate mergers and takeovers, and changing business strategies. But amid all these changes there is also continuity. The corporate elite is, in Italian elite theorist Gaetano Mosca's words, an "organized minority" that generates its own power effect by bringing the top capitalists and their advisors into an integrated "small world." As the title of this book implies, it is the corporate elite that organizes the 1%. Even as capitalists struggle among themselves for shares of the total surplus value that is continuously being appropriated from workers, a cohesive corporate community instils in its members a collective consciousness and a culture of class solidarity. In this sense, as we argue below, the corporate elite is foundational to capitalist class hegemony.[2]

RECENT CHANGES IN THE CANADIAN CORPORATE ELITE

In Chapter 2 we showed how, a century ago, the Canadian corporate elite had already emerged through three processes: (1) the concentration and centralization of capital into large corporations and banks, (2) the integration of industrial and financial capital as finance capital and (3) the elaboration of a dense network of interlocking corporate directorates. The elite, and its power, were further consolidated in the middle decades of the twentieth century, within a system of "organized capitalism" that involved a class compromise. By 1980, sociologist Michael Ornstein characterized the corporate-interlock network in Canada as one of the most integrated of all the advanced capitalist formations. Beginning in the late twentieth century, increased capitalist globalization and the turn to market-driven politics meant a shift to neoliberal globalization, which "disorganized" some of the aspects of corporations and the state.[3]

In the era of organized capitalism, from the early to late twentieth century, the centres of finance — the chartered banks — maintained stable relations with their corporate partners. These relations were often cemented in interlocking directorates that gave bankers direct representation on the boards of their major clients. To maintain the financial system's stability, chartered banks were not allowed to function as investment banks (that is, to deal in corporate shares and securities) and were restricted to commercial and consumer lending. However, in 1987 the federal government allowed chartered banks to become investment dealers, meaning they could deal in corporate shares and other tradeable securities in great quantity. This began a transition in which banks' balance sheets were recomposed. Although loans continue to be an important component of bank assets, the proportion of corporate shares and other tradeable securities has greatly increased. This shift from the "patient money" of long-term loans to transaction-based finance has weakened the institutional relations between banks and their corporate clients. As those relations become more transactional, there is less of a need for banks to be represented on the boards of corporate clients and oversee their long-term investments.[4]

Yet, as we saw in the previous chapter, banks and other centres of financial power remain important, though they now wield power within a more globalized economic framework. A key finding from research on changes to the Canadian corporate elite's structure in the late twentieth century is that although the corporations at the network's centre became more transnationally invested, an integrated national elite remained in place at the core of corporate power: "'Transnational finance capital' has radiated from Canada in a way that has *not* disorganized the national network, but has *embedded* it more extensively in a circuitry of global accumulation." Sociologist Jamie Brownlee adds, "For the most part, the Canadian network has remained domestic in terms of its locus of control and retained a predominantly national base." The coming of "disorganized" and globalized capitalism did not disorganize Canada's corporate elite, but it did extend that elite's transnational reach while weakening the institutionalized ties between banks and industry.[5]

Although the corporate elite is primarily a condensation of class power, other aspects of social power are also elemental to it. A key issue in the study of elites is "closure," or "the process by which social collectivities seek to maximize rewards by restricting access to resources and opportunities to a limited circle of eligibles," as British sociologist Frank Parkin once put it. Such privilege is secured at the expense of the excluded groups, which in Canada have been made up of ethnic minorities, Indigenous peoples and women. At the core of the corporate elite were a few dozen "big linkers," each holding at least four major corporate directorships, who comprised an elite within the elite. In the mid-1970s, the elite (each holding at least two dominant directorships) was overwhelmingly white Anglo-Saxon Protestant (WASP) and male. This began to change slightly in the late twentieth century. The elite network became less centralized as the number of big linkers fell from 128 to 82 between 1976 and 1996. Women gained a toehold (rising from 0.6 percent of the elite to 9.2 percent), and the dominance of the British ethnic group declined (although by 1996 less than one percent of the corporate elite had origins outside of Europe, and none was of Indigenous ancestry). These shifts were far from seismic. But they did make the corporate elite a little more multicultural (in a Eurocentric way) and a little less patriarchal, while weakening the highly exclusive old boys' network.[6]

What changed less in the same time period was the class composition of the corporate elite. Throughout, roughly one-tenth of the elite were major shareholders in a dominant corporation, and most of the rest were executives either in a dominant firm or in a smaller company. One broad category did expand (at the expense of the various executives): In 1976, 20.4 percent of the elite were outside directors of dominant corporations, without any executive position or major shareholdings. That is, they were advisors to the capitalist class. By 1996, the complement of advisors had grown to 27.4 percent, largely on account of the increasing numbers of retired capitalists (*éminence grise*), consultants and academics serving on multiple corporate boards. Such advisors, comprising more than a quarter of the elite, play an important role. They are not themselves active capitalists with major stakes in the firms they direct, but, as Jorge Niosi observed, are "organic intellectuals" — lawyers, accountants, academics, retired politicians and other well-placed or highly skilled individuals who provide crucial technical expertise and experience, sometimes to several large firms. Such advisors and functionaries make up an important stratum of the corporate elite, one that exercises not only economic power, but also cultural and political leadership, or, in other words, hegemony.[7]

Table 5.1. The corporate elite is composed
of capitalists and their advisors[8]

Class Position	1976	1996
Active capitalists		
Major shareholder in a Top 250 firm	9.2%	10.6%
President/CEO of a Top 250 firm	21.9%	17.9%
Other executive in a Top 250 firm	12.1%	7.5%
Chair of a Top 250 firm	5.3%	6.6%
Executive or proprietor in a smaller firm	31.1%	30.1%
Organic intellectuals		
Éminence grise	2.9%	6.8%
Legal advisor	10.8%	9.9%
Consultant	3.1%	4.9%
Academic advisor	1.0%	3.5%
State official	1.4%	0.9%
Other advisor	1.2%	1.2%
Total	100.0%	100.0%

CORPORATE POWER AND HEGEMONY

As the leading edge of a dominant class, the corporate elite expresses more than an assortment of economic interests chasing profit. Of course, in pursuing maximum profit for a given firm, members of the elite relate to each other in instrumental terms, as means towards that particular end. But they are also bound together as leading members of a dominant class. The elite's material source of power — its control over concentrations of capital and thus economic surplus — is not its only power resource. The corporate elite is also a staging ground of cultural and political leadership. Its hegemony consists in exercising that leadership beyond the world of corporate business, reaching into civil society and the state. It is this modality of power that enables the capitalist class to act on its collective interests, or what Marx called as a class for itself. The corporate elite is a crucial element in the exercise of such power. Here again, social organization figures significantly. If the corporate elite were fragmented into warring groups, there would be no structural basis for capitalist class hegemony. By contrast, a cohesive, socially integrated corporate elite can reach a consensus on long-term goals and vision. With that, it can speak politically with a single voice, and lead.[9]

Hegemony is not about the brute dominance of capitalists over other interests in society. Indeed, naked dominance is, as political theorist Antonio Gramsci insisted, the opposite of hegemony. The class hegemony in which the corporate elite participates is an ongoing accomplishment of business leadership, which includes the absorption of leaders and ideas from other spheres into the world of corporate business. That requires persuasion, not coercion. Hegemony is rule with the consent of the governed, but *consent does not necessarily mean democracy*. There is a deep-seated contradiction between the democratic practices of self-governance and the rule of corporate capital, however effective the latter might be in organizing the consent of subordinate groups. Capitalist hegemony is about muting that contradiction and constructing common-sense truths to fill the gap between democratic aspiration and the lived reality of class inequality.[10]

In Table 5.2 we summarize the various modalities of corporate power. The middle column shows the three economic modalities, which we analyzed in Chapters 3 and 4. The right-hand column identifies two distinct modalities of *class hegemony*, which we analyze here and in the next chapter. The first of these resides in the internal structure of the corporate elite. That structure — its cohesion as a well-integrated network, inclusive of various capitalist interests — nurtures a close-knit corporate community. Frequent interaction builds up a fund of common experiences, a shared vision of the world and a collective consciousness. Interlocking directorships enable elite integration, even if social cohesion is no more than an unintended consequence of interlocking. So, according to sociologists John Porter and Wallace Clement, do elite private clubs, residential segregation within elite neighbourhoods and other devices of social closure and elite solidarity.

Table 5.2. Forms, agents, and sites of corporate power[11]

	Economy	Political and civil society
Forms	Power exercised as capital *accumulation*: operational, strategic, and allocative power	Power exercised as *hegemony*: elite integration (cohesion), business leadership in politics and culture (reach)
Agents	Top executives, major shareholders (individual and institutional), bankers, with assistance of technical experts	Organic intellectuals, including capitalists involved in business leadership
Sites	Internal management structures; corporate directorates; directorates of financial institutions, pension funds, investment companies	Corporate directorates, private clubs, policy-planning groups, industry associations, lobbies, university governance boards, revolving doors, etc.

Complementing the cohesion that promotes elite solidarity, the second hegemonic modality of corporate power is reach into the public sphere. There are many means by which corporate power extends in this way, and the traffic is by no means one-way. Via "revolving doors" between corporations and the state, the flow of corporate capitalists into government is reciprocated by the migration of retiring politicians into the corporate elite. This two-way traffic is important in itself. It is not unusual for capitalists themselves to exercise cultural and political leadership, wielding economic power while contributing to the construction of hegemony, or temporarily shifting from the world of business to political leadership. For example, investment banker Joe Oliver worked for Merrill Lynch and Nesbitt Thomson before he ran for office with the Conservative Party and served as Stephen Harper's Finance Minister. Canada's current Finance Minister, businessman Bill Morneau, was executive chair of human resources company Morneau Shepell, and he also chaired the C.D. Howe Institute.

Nevertheless, the capitalist class's hegemony relies heavily on the agency of organic intellectuals who are not themselves capitalists. Such individuals take up support roles in the world of business — often as advisors or consultants — yet they are organizers of culture and politics. The corporate elite's hegemonic reach depends on a vast range of such organizers and knowledge-producers in think tanks, industry and lobby groups, media and higher education, who exercise leadership in policy-planning, lobbying, news and commentary, and university governance. We will map out this "reach" in the next chapter. Here, we want to focus on the overall network of corporate affiliations and its contribution to elite cohesion.

As Jamie Brownlee, drawing on the work of fellow sociologist Michael Useem, points out, three aspects of interlocking directorates make them effective as conduits of power for the corporate elite:

> First, the bulk of their members are fulltime senior managers of large corporations. Second, the network of directorates includes almost all of the large, dominant companies. And third, the ties are dispersed in a fashion that favours class-wide integration.

The network of interlocking directorates pulls together leading capitalists and organic intellectuals, as a corporate community. Many studies have examined the Canadian corporate elite from this network angle. As we mentioned in Chapter 2, the network was already quite developed a century ago, and became increasingly integrated yet differentiated in the decades following World War Two.[12]

In fact, some of the relationships between dominant corporations were remarkably stable across many decades. Over the post-war era, twenty-one major corporations exchanged multiple directors with each other, on an ongoing basis. Eight of them, including the Bank of Montreal, Royal Bank of Canada, Sun Life and CPR, were members of the main financial group that Gilles Piédalue mapped as of 1930. And the CPR-Bank of Montreal interlock was particularly strong and durable. Gilles Piédalue found that these two bedrock institutions of Canadian finance capital shared five directors as early as 1910. Between 1946 and1976, they averaged seven shared directors per year! As one of us concluded in 1986, these foundational corporate-elite relations "have been at the centre of Canadian monopoly capital for most of this century."[13]

Comparatively, Canada's corporate elite is highly cohesive. Sociologist Michael Ornstein compared the 1980 Canadian network of interlocking directorates with corporate networks in Austria, Belgium, Britain, Finland, France, Germany, Italy, the Netherlands, Switzerland and the United States, focusing in each case on the fifty largest financial institutions and the 200 largest non-financials. He found that the five big banks stood out as key sites of network integration, averaging eighty-four interlocks, compared to the five most heavily interlocked non-financials, which average fifty-five ties. Canada's network contained the largest number of big linkers. Ornstein concluded that "in Canada, there is a very cohesive network, which is tied together by a relatively small number of individuals with many board positions ... lend[ing] support to the models of capitalist class relations which emphasize unity." A similar study by William Carroll and Malcolm Alexander compared the Top 250 corporations of Canada and Australia as of 1992. They found that companies in Canada are three times more likely to interlock with each other than companies in Australia. When they focused on the interlocks created by the multiple affiliations of outside directors, the difference was even sharper. The study thus indicates that the Canadian corporate elite gains some of its cohesion from the extensive participation of organic intellectuals on multiple corporate boards.[14]

More recently, one of us has collaborated with political scientist Jerome Klassen, in two studies tracing changes in the Canadian corporate elite between 1996 and 2006. In the first study we addressed the issue of whether corporate Canada is being "hollowed out" through the increasing dominance of foreign, and particularly U.S.-based, corporations. Legal scholar Harry Arthurs had advanced this thesis in 2000. He claimed that as foreign parent companies tighten their operational control of Canadian subsidiaries, "the community of directors and senior executives of Canadian domestic corporations and foreign-owned subsidiaries – is being 'hollowed out.'"[15]

To check into this, we examined the Canadian Top 250 network of 1996 and 2006. To highlight change over the decade we tracked each firm as to whether it numbered among the Top 250 in both years ("top dogs"), disappeared from the Top 250 after 1996 ("fallen angels") or entered the Top 250 as of 2006 ("rising stars"). In effect, the rising stars, 120 fast-growing corporations, replace the 120 fallen angels as they disappear due to takeovers, bankruptcies or a slow rate of accumulation. "Hollowing out" implies a decline in the control of corporate Canada by domestic capitalists. But as of 2006, 81 percent of the 130 top dog corporations were controlled in Canada, 12 percent were controlled in the U.S. and 8 percent were controlled elsewhere. Among the 120 rising stars, 77 percent were controlled in Canada, 8 percent in the U.S. and 16 percent elsewhere. So Canadian capitalists continue to predominate in the corporate elite, as the composition of leading corporations changed, while the presence of U.S.-based capital has waned and the presence of other transnational capital has waxed. These trends are more consistent with the multilateral internationalization of capital, which is not specific to Canada but has been happening all over, including in the U.S.[16]

For the Canadian corporate elite as a community, a key question is whether the rising stars actually replace the fallen angels in the corporate network, or whether the network is being hollowed out, or is falling apart. We found that top dogs controlled by Canadian capitalists were especially central in the network in both years, forming the network core. Rising stars under Canadian control had become highly central by 2006, showing many interlocks with the Canadian-controlled top dog companies. However, the American-based corporations (which in 1996 were very weakly linked into the network) became almost entirely detached. From all this, we concluded that

> for the Canadian segment of the elite, just as the accumulation of capital provides for a replenishment of Canada-based corporate capital, with fallen angels replaced by rising stars, the elite is continually recomposed as the latter are integrated into the network. In this way, *capital accumulation and social organization intersect in the reproduction of a domestic corporate community.* In this process of elite reproduction, top dogs play an important role, linking mainly with each other but also with rising stars.

In short, "the Canadian corporate community is more resilient than posited under the thesis of hollowing out."[17]

In our second study, we examined the developing interlocks between Canada's corporate community and the global corporate elite. We chose the 250 largest Canada-based companies and tracked their interlocks with each other and with the largest 500 corporations in the world in 1996 and 2006. Over that decade, many of Canada's top corporations became more transnational in their investment reach, while companies that remained purely domestic in their investments participated less in the national corporate community. We found that "globalizing firms are increasingly dominant in the national network, *and* increasingly integrated with the transnational network of corporate power," as the centre of gravity of the "national" network became increasingly transnational. Canada's corporate elite had not been hollowed out, but was becoming increasingly inhabited by transnational firms based in Canada, which link up with other TNCs on a global scale, forming "the rudiments of a transnational capitalist class."[18]

Figure 5.1 provides a finance-centred snapshot of the network as of yearend 2016. It includes the five largest Canadian banks plus two major financial institutions (discussed in Chapter 4) and maps the web of relationships they are embedded in through interlocking boards of directors. In this "two mode" representation of the network, we can see how directors and executives (white circles) affiliated with multiple corporations (diamonds, squares and other shapes) link companies together. The figure first suggests a tightly connected network among the country's top financial institutions: despite that banks are prohibited by Canadian law to share directors, we see that most of them have directors who meet on the boards of other large corporations. Large financial institutions are thus connected indirectly through a small number of individual members of the corporate elite. For example, Royal Bank of Canada (RBC) director David P. Denison is also a director of Ontario power utility Hydro One, where he meets with Jane Peverett from CIBC. Denison also meets CIBC's Martine Turcotte when he attends BCE board meetings, where he is likewise in contact with Sophie Brochu and George A. Cope, both directors of the Bank of Montreal. The Bank of Nova Scotia (ScotiaBank) similarly connects to RBC through chemical producer Potash Corporation of Saskatchewan[19] and heavy machinery distributor Finnings International. The network neighbouring Canada's largest financial institutions thus appears to be tightly integrated through interlocking directorates.

A second observation is that the Canadian network extends beyond national borders, mainly to the United States (U.S. corporations are shown in dark grey on the figure) and to Europe (shown in light grey). As explained, even though its centre of gravity still is nationally based, the Canadian corporate community has been transnationalized to a great extent. This takes place as Canadian executives serve on foreign boards, such as Paul Desmarais Jr., who is on the boards of Swiss-French cement producer LafargeHolcim and French oil and gas major Total. Conversely, some foreign executives come into the Canadian community, such as Bridget van Kralingen, senior vice president at IBM, or Thomas

Figure 5.1. Interlocks among seven large Canadian financial institutions and other large corporations [20]

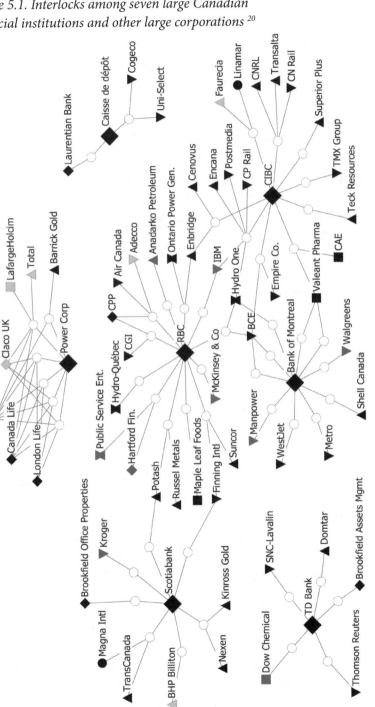

A. Renyi, retired CEO of the Bank of New York Mellon, who both sit on RBC's board.

The two-mode representation emphasizes the dual nature of the corporate network. In the network, corporate boards are meeting sites where individual capitalists meet, plan strategy and exert their allocative, strategic and organizational power as agents of capital accumulation. Additionally, as explained above, by fostering social cohesion among the corporate elite, corporate boards also enable agency in the political and cultural fields, where their power is exerted as hegemony. We will discuss this aspect at greater length in the next chapter.

Notwithstanding its high cohesiveness, the corporate elite contains subgroups and "fractions" that are also worth examining. We recently mapped the "carbon-capital elite" that is nested within the larger Canadian corporate community. Focusing on the 238 largest Canada-based firms in the oil/gas/coal sector, we find a tightly-knit, Calgary-based network of mid-sized carbon-capital firms. This network links into the broader power structure through interlocks involving the largest carbon-capital corporations. Those carbon majors tend to interlock more widely, not only with other Canadian carbon-capital firms but also with Canada's major financial institutions and other industrial firms, as well as with corporations based outside of Canada. The network is national, but it has a regional geography:

> Corporate power's spatial organization concentrates command over carbon resources largely in Calgary, while financial and other corporations are based in Toronto and to a lesser extent Montreal and Vancouver. Directorate interlocks stitch corporations into a national elite network. In its transnational connections (where the carbon majors are especially active), the network is concentrated largely within the North Atlantic zone of the global economy, the heartland for a transnational capitalist class.[21]

This entire raft of research findings confirms the continued existence of an integrated corporate elite in Canada. Within this corporate community power is centralized, as top capitalists and their advisors interact frequently, maintaining a sense of solidarity and common purpose even as they compete over the division of spoils appropriated from labour. As we have seen, interlocking directorates are vehicles for coordinated capital accumulation (within financial groups, for example), but they are also expressions of class hegemony, enabling the capitalist class to rule.

Yet there are other kinds of social relations that also bolster that hegemony. Classically, elite private clubs played an important role in cementing the "old boys club," as sociologist John Porter found in the 1950s, and as Wallace Clement reported in the 1970s. In those years, clubs based mainly in Montreal and Toronto were exclusive places where members of the corporate elite could socialize apart from executive suites and boardrooms. It was not uncommon for a member of the elite to belong to three or four clubs in his city of residence. In 1954, as Porter found, Montreal's Mount Royal Club alone included 150 members of Canada's corporate elite (comprising 34.5 percent of its membership) while the Toronto Club included 105. By 1996, the clubs had emptied out to some extent. Only 32 members of the elite belonged to the Mount Royal Club, while the Toronto Club included 51 (with 24 members of the elite belonging to both these clubs). The clubs still served as meeting points, but for a much reduced complement of the corporate elite.[22]

However, just as the globalization of capital has not brought the hollowing out of Corporate Canada, the relative decline of private clubs as a source of elite integration did not signify a weakening in overall integration. In the same years that club membership dropped, Canada's corporate elite began to fund and govern a growing number of policy-planning organizations. Corporate-supported think tanks and business councils have become crucial sites not only of elite integration but of "business activism."

In the popular imagination, activism is identified with visible protest, often in the streets. But given its superior power resources, the corporate elite's activism takes a less visible form. Corporate-supported think tanks and business councils produce a steady stream of pro-business policy perspectives, under the strategic direction of governance boards laden with members of the corporate elite. As sociologist Michael Useem found in the U.S. and U.K., such elite activism was critical in developing the neoliberal policy framework in the 1970s and 1980s. For Canada's corporate community, what was striking in the period from the 1970s to the 1990s was "the extent to which the cultural basis for elite solidarity shifted from the sphere of leisure to that of activism." This shift, from private clubs to policy-planning as a key preoccupation for the elite outside of the world of business, brings us to the topic of our next chapter: corporate capital's reach into political and civil society.[23]

Chapter 6

WHEN IDEAS BECOME COMMON SENSE

The Corporate Reach Into Culture and Politics

Corporate power reaches into civil and political society in multiple ways. In each instance, the interests of corporations and capitalists are presented as the "general interests" of everyone. After all, most everyone wants a job, income, a measure of prosperity and so on. And the investment decisions of corporations and capitalists determine whether, where and for whom these beneficial outcomes will occur. So, especially where people lack any alternative narrative for making sense of the situation (for instance, a critical analysis of capitalism as a system of exploitation and colonization), business interests (to maximize profit through largely unrestricted investment) masquerade as societal interests. The idea is that some of the wealth at the top trickles down to the bottom, so everyone is better off. When such ideas become "common sense," corporate power achieves a strong hegemony. Such was the case in the U.S. in 1953, at the height of Cold War anti-communism, when General Motors CEO Charles Erwin Wilson said in response to questions about conflict of interest during his confirmation hearing to become Secretary of Defense: "For years I thought what was good for the country was good for General Motors and vice versa." (Later this was shortened to "What's good for General Motors is good for the country.")[1]

However, counter-narratives are popping up all the time, often through the efforts of grassroots social movements contesting corporate power and the "trickle-down economics" that legitimate it. This is a topic we will cover in the conclusion, but the point here is that corporate power does face challenges from below, which is why it needs to maintain a strong presence in the organizations and institutions of civil society and the state. The corporate elite needs to win the hearts and minds of the people (and the state managers), on an ongoing basis. In a way of life deeply marked by class inequality and deepening ecological crisis, the corporate elite must struggle to maintain its hegemony.

Thus, corporate power reaches beyond the economy, as business leadership, into civil and political society. As it reaches, it recruits support for a worldview in which capital's particular interest in profitable accumulation, often phrased for the general public simply as "jobs," becomes universalized. To reach effectively, to be a leading hegemonic force, the corporate elite must achieve and maintain a certain social cohesiveness as a business community. It needs an internal basis of solidarity, built through frequent interaction, and shared perspectives on what is to be done. We saw in Chapter 5 that the network of interlocking corporate directorships provides the infrastructure for such cohesiveness. Simultaneously, allocative power reaches from the economy into other fields. Funds accumulated as capital are selectively directed, often through foundations, to policy-planning groups, political parties, lobbies and industry groups, universities and research centres and more.

We can present the various modalities of corporate power graphically by returning to John Urry's description of capitalist society as the overlapping fields of economy, civil society and state. Within the economy, as we saw in Chapters 3 and 4, corporate power is stitched into the very process of accumulating capital. It appears as strategic control of companies, allocative power over funds and operational power within firms and across commodity chains. The corporate community achieves its cohesiveness in a space between economy and civil society, through networks that may be grounded in economy (interlocking directorates) or civil society (such as private clubs).

A cohesive corporate elite can speak with one voice, and lead. Figure 6.1 further specifies the hegemonic modalities of corporate power, as influence reaches from the corporate sector into civil society and the state in multiple ways. Vis-à-vis civil society, these include:

- business activism and leadership exercised by corporate elites,

Figure 6.1. Modalities of corporate power

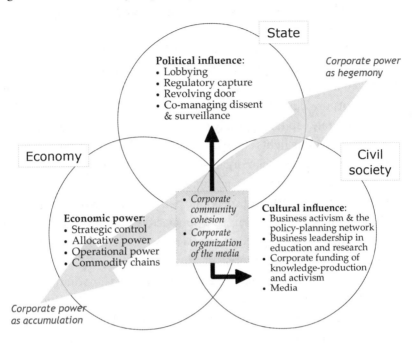

- funding relationships that empower think tanks, advocacy groups and political parties,
- corporate social responsibility (CSR) and public-relations (PR) initiatives,
- the framing of news content to privilege business interests, and
- the corporate organization of communications media themselves.

Corporate power reaches into the state via relations and practices that include lobbying, regulatory capture, revolving doors and the co-management of dissent in partnership with social control authorities.

CORPORATE REACH INTO CIVIL SOCIETY

Corporate power reaches into civil and political society with generally injurious effects on democracy. At the core of a vibrant democracy is an ongoing public conversation in which all with a stake in an issue have a say. As corporate power reaches into the public sphere, it distorts communication, privileging the perspectives and interests of those who own and control capital. A raft of Canadian studies, inspired by John Porter, has mapped the intricate ties that bring business leadership into the cultural fields.[2]

In many cases, this influence takes the form of interlocking directorates between large corporations and organizations in three sectors of civil society. First, there are organizations whose objective is to define and advance corporate interests. These organizations are the direct political arm of corporate capital. Typically they are sponsored by corporate business, and the leading lights of big business grace their governance boards. There are two kinds of such organizations: industry associations, which advocate for specific industries, and intersectoral business councils, which construct and advance broad corporate perspectives across sectors. Both kinds develop policy proposals and perspectives and promote them via various media, including reports, media releases, social media initiatives, advertising, lobbying and more.[3]

Sectoral industry associations, such as the Canadian Bankers Association and the Canadian Association of Petroleum Producers, are places where fractional interests are defined and advanced. On specific issues the immediate interests of one fraction (for example, coal) may conflict with those of another (for example, natural gas is typically promoted as a transition fuel in the sun-setting of coal). Thus, even if the Canadian Gas Association and the Coal Association of Canada disagree on specific policies, corporate members of both organizations participate together in hammering out a wider collective interest within intersectoral groups, such as the deregulation of energy projects assessment.[4]

For their part, intersectoral business councils and chambers of commerce represent corporate capital's broad class interests. The most influential intersectoral organization has been the Business Council of Canada (BCC), which since the 1980s has significantly shaped the neoliberal policy paradigm. Indeed, according to Jamie Brownlee, the BCC "may be unique in the developed world in terms of its capacity to dominate political life." As BCC CEO Thomas d'Aquino concluded a couple of decades ago in an interview with journalist Peter Newman:

> If you ask yourself, in which period since 1900 has Canada's business community had the most influence on public policy, I would say it was the last twenty years. Look at what we stand for and

look at what all the governments, all the major parties ... have done, and what they want to do. They have adopted the agendas we've been fighting for in the past two decades.[5]

Current BCC CEO, John Manley, exemplifies the revolving door between the state and corporate sectors. Initially a tax lawyer, he entered federal politics in the 1980s and was a key cabinet minister in the Liberal governments of 1993–2004. Upon retiring from politics, he joined a number of corporate directorates, including the Canadian Imperial Bank of Commerce. In 2010 he became CEO of the BCC. Never an actual capitalist, Manley continues to be an important organic intellectual of the capitalist class, helping to organize and define its class interests and perspectives, while serving on several corporate directorates.

A second kind of civil-society organization, one that is less immediately tied to corporate capital and less focused on defining and defending business interests per se, is the policy-planning group, or think tank. Such groups are politically nonpartisan and formally autonomous from the corporate sector. But research reviewed by Jamie Brownlee has shown them to be funded by large corporations and directed by their CEOs. In comparison to industry associations and business councils, think tanks are organizations of professional researchers, analysts and communicators. They focus not on defining and advancing corporate interests but on producing evidence-based commentary and analysis from a standpoint compatible with business interests. Think tanks are typically non-profit organizations, self-defined as "educational organizations, committed to increased public awareness about policy issues," as Brownlee has observed. In the policy-planning process, think tanks deploy their paid staff of researchers and communications experts, along with academics who share a commitment to business-friendly policy. At the same time, they connect with governmental and media personnel, through workshops, conferences and fora. Through this corporate-laden policy-planning network, the corporate elite's vision and policy preferences are elaborated and presented by seemingly "independent" experts. Power structure analyst William Domhoff explains how this works:

The policy-planning network explains how seemingly independent experts, who often provide new policy ideas, fit into the power equation. They do their work as employees and consultants of key organizations in the network, which give them financial support, confer legitimacy on their efforts, and provide the occasions for them to present their ideas to decision-makers.[6]

Among the most important think tanks in Canada are Toronto-based C.D. Howe Institute (CDHI) and Vancouver-based Fraser Institute. Widely seen as Canada's most influential think tank, the C.D. Howe Institute received major donations from coal giant Atco, from Power Corporation and from Peter Munk, founder and chairman of Barrick Gold, among others.[7] CDHI describes itself as "a trusted source of essential policy intelligence, distinguished by research that is nonpartisan, evidence-based and subject to definitive expert review." Indeed, in reviewing its own political impact, CDHI boasts of having "laid the intellectual ground" for such "fundamental achievements" as continental free trade, deficit-reduction as a state priority, a low-tax regime and other core elements of neoliberalism. The Fraser Institute, founded a year after CDHI in 1974, has been a leading force in advancing the neoliberal corporate agenda in Canada. Very little is known about the institute's funders, though their 2016 annual report mentions a one-time $5 million donation by mining baron Peter Munk,[8] and it has been reported the Institute received recurring donations from the fossil fuel billionaire Koch brothers at least between 2007 and 2012.[9] Ranked in 2016 as the top think tank in Canada and nineteenth out of nearly seven thousand think tanks around the world by a University of Pennsylvania research team, the Fraser Institute is a longstanding core member of the Atlas Network, an interconnected collection of 450 right-wing think tanks in over ninety countries. Its policy work is carried out by a staff of twelve researchers and a group of sixty-nine "Senior Fellows," most of whom are academics at universities in Canada and elsewhere. In addition to policy work, the Fraser Institute provides extensive programming in "education," conveying the gospel of free markets, deregulation and privatization to students, teachers and journalists through seminars, internships, workshops and other initiatives.[10]

A third kind of civil-society organization, and the kind most distant from direct corporate control, is the non-profit organization. This diverse category includes charities and philanthropic foundations, hospitals, various non-governmental organizations and universities. Each has its own governance board, offering the prospect of high-level participation from

the corporate elite. In these instances, corporate power is at its most dif-
fuse. The point is not to advance a specific business agenda, but to offer
leadership from a standpoint that emphasizes a corporate worldview.
While the corporate presence on hospital boards and foundations has
been well documented by sociologists John Fox, Michael Ornstein and
Jamie Brownlee, we will restrict our discussion here to the interesting case
of universities. As part of the neoliberal agenda, universities have been
increasingly "corporatized" since the 1980s. This process is multifaceted,
and elite interlocks give us just a small fragment of the big picture.[11]

Corporate power within institutions of higher education has grown
as public funding of universities and research has shrunk. In the three
decades following 1979, state funding fell from 84 percent of Canadian
universities' budgets to 58 percent. With declining public revenue, "universities are increasingly managed as entrepreneurial institutions, and
corporate influence over the terms of the university-business relationship
deepens," according to sociologists William Carroll, Nicolas Graham
and Zoë Yunker. But corporate influence has deep roots. In 1906, as
sociologist Jamie Brownlee recounts, the newly implemented University
Act "placed control and management of the University of Toronto in the
hands of an appointed body, the Board of Governors, which consisted
largely of wealthy business leaders." This corporate university model was
then repeated at other Canadian universities, giving rise to an extensive
network of elite affiliations crossing between the worlds of corporate
business and academe, as sociologists William Carroll and James Beaton
found. In the later decades of the twentieth century, public funding cuts
led universities to launch massive fundraising campaigns, increasing the
value of corporate representation on university boards. Business journalist
Trevor Cole reported that by 1998 the University of Toronto had offset its
15.3 percent cut in funding with a $400 million campaign, spearheaded by
executives from leading Canadian corporations. Meanwhile, according to
the Canadian Association of University Teachers, funding of research by
corporations and wealthy individuals has been sharply rising and reshap-
ing the universities that host (and effectively subsidize) these activities. As
noted in a recent report, "When wealthy donors fund a new program or
centre, they often want a voice in academic matters like hiring, awarding
of scholarships and faculty choices in research.[12]

When we map interlocking directorates between the major Canadian corporations we examined in Chapter 5 and a select group of civil-society organizations, we find a densely connected network 2 (Figure 6.2). We have selected just two universities as illustrative cases: McGill and the University of Toronto. We also illustrate three corporate-led policy-planning groups and think tanks: the Business Council of Canada (BCC), the C.D. Howe Institute and the Fraser Institute; and one industry group, the Canadian Association of Petroleum Producers (CAPP), the main association and lobby group of the oil and gas industry. Corporations are shown as circles; triangles represent policy-planning groups and think tanks; and diamonds represent the main banks and financial institutions discussed in Chapter 5. Financial corporations are shown in black; mining, manufacturing, transportation sectors are in light grey; and service, retail and wholesale industries are in dark grey. Node size indicates corporate revenue.

At the very core of this network are the BCC and the C.D. Howe Institute, who bring an extensive number of companies together and thus account for a great part of the cohesiveness of the Canadian corporate community. The Fraser Institute plays a similar role, though to a lesser extent. This illustrates the key role these nominally independent policy-planning groups and think tanks play in elaborating and disseminating ideas on behalf of the corporate elite, whose members steer and fund them. Additionally, the extent of their reach across economic sectors and regions enables them to develop a true class perspective that transcends narrow interests, thus constructing a sense of a general interest of the corporate community. In this way, the elite is able to present unified positions to policy-makers, allowing greater effectiveness on policy issues. As an industry association, the CAPP plays a similar role among the oil and gas sector and links a large portion of the sector together. Although many smaller firms do not appear on the above figure, it is one of the functions of CAPP to provide a forum where different interests of smaller and larger firms can be bridged.

As explained above, universities are key locations for the exercise of corporate hegemony, which is illustrated by their position in the web of intercorporate relationships. Several corporate executives sit on the board of McGill University. For example, Claude Généreux is an executive at Power Corp and is also a board member of the Rhodes Scholarship of Canada; Martine Turcotte is a vice-president at BCE and is a director of CIBC and Empire Co. (Sobeys); and Thierry Vandal, CEO of Hydro-Québec from 2005 to 2015, sits on the board of the Royal Bank of Canada (RBC).

Figure 6.2. Interlocks between the largest Canadian corporations and civil society organizations

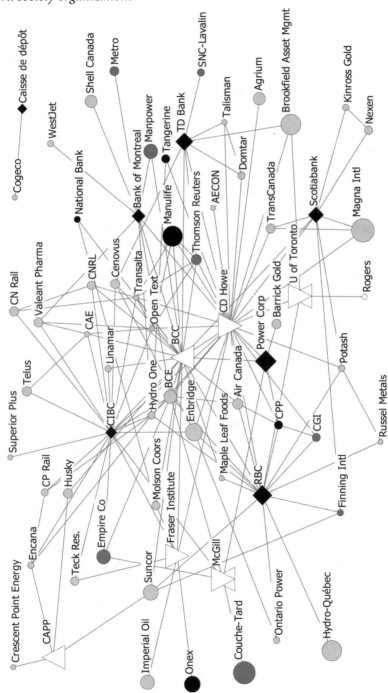

The board of the University of Toronto is similarly staffed: Melinda Rogers is deputy chair of Rogers Communications and a member of the fourth wealthiest family in Canada in 2017. Janet Ecker, Ontario Minister of Finance from 2002–03, also sits on the board of the C.D. Howe Institute. Fellow C.D. Howe board member Brian K. Johnstone is a Toronto-area real estate executive, Chief Operating Officer of Mattamy Homes and member of the board of the Mortgage Company of Canada. Brian Lawson is the chief financial officer of the major financial firm Brookfield Asset Management, and he also chairs the Trinity College School Foundation. Finally, University of Toronto Governing Council member Zabeen Hirji was in charge of human resources at RBC before retiring at the end of 2017.

Connections between other major universities and very large corporations often take place through business schools' advisory boards, onto which members of the corporate elite are invited, oftentimes as large donors to the school. In the neoliberal model of higher education, institutions increasingly depend on corporate donations to fund their activities. In this way, the presence of prominent capitalists on their boards helps attract wealthy donors. Corporate donations provide a direct conduit for the exercise of allocative power. Again in this case, this power works not so much by shaping higher education curriculum as through donor companies' capacity to withdraw funding in the case of decisions going counter their general and particular interests.

CORPORATE REACH INTO THE STATE

As studies reviewed in the previous chapter have shown, the elite network through which corporate power reaches into key organizations of civil society was instrumental in championing the neoliberal agenda, from the early 1980s forward. In our current era, the network continues to provide important channels for political activism by business executives and high-level corporate influence within organizations and institutions of civil society. But there are other no less important forms of corporate reach.[13]

Large corporations (and their representatives in industry associations and business councils) are by far the main lobbyists at federal and provincial levels. For instance, between 2011 and early 2016, CAPP alone lobbied the federal government 1,015 times — nearly on a daily basis. The Business Council of Canada logged 370 such events. The Canadian

National Railway lobbied 864 times; TransCanada Corporation lobbied 587 times, and the Canadian Gas Association 477 times. In these frequent meetings, corporations and industry groups use both in-house staff and specialist lobbying organizations to influence the broad strokes as well as the fine details of policy. Corporate capital is unique in the vast resources (including battalions of organic intellectuals) it dedicates to this form of paid political influence.[14]

The same kinds of relationships are in play at the provincial level. Sociologist Nicolas Graham and his colleagues tracked lobbying events in British Columbia involving the top ten fossil fuel companies between 2010 and 2016. These organizations, which accounted for three-quarters of all lobbying in that economic sector, reported a total of 19,517 lobbying contacts with B.C. public office holders, making an average of fourteen per business day. In comparison, environmental nongovernmental organizations like Greenpeace lobbied infrequently. There were only eight such organizations, reporting 1,324 contacts in total. Moreover, among the corporate players there was a substantial overlap between lobbying and donations to the governing Liberal Party of B.C. Seven of the top ten political donors ranked among the top ten lobbyists. Most of the corporate donations (92 percent of more than $5 million) were directed to the pro-business Liberals. As Nicolas Graham, Shannon Daub and William Carroll conclude:

> The purchasing of access to key politicians is complemented by and often works in concert with the lobbying process, which seeks to establish close links with government officials and torque policy and political decision-making in favour of the fossil fuel industry. Reflecting the concentration of corporate power in a small number of entities, most of the lobbying in the sector occurs within a tight network of top corporations, industry groups and government bodies. The same holds for political donations, which are funnelled toward the B.C. Liberals, with the NDP collecting what amounts to chump change. As top lobbyists and political donors, the fossil fuel industry enjoys access to provincial decision-makers that everyday citizens and public-interest organizations can only dream about.[15]

Another mechanism of corporate reach into the state is the "revolving door" between business and the state. As political economist Leo Panitch observed in the 1970s, capitalists have long held close relationships with the Canadian state. For instance, David Nock's study of federal cabinets and Senate members revealed that throughout the twentieth century "the frequency of politicians obtaining business positions or of businessmen entering political life, is so common that the two institutional sectors may be better visualized as two intersecting circles with substantial degree of overlap, rather than as two separate circles." Nock found many instances of revolving doors, flows of leaders to and from the corporate elite and top state bodies. But more worrisome are the many *simultaneous* affiliations, or interlocks, between the corporate sector and the Senate. In effect, the Senate has long been and still is an unelected repository for the corporate elite's *éminence grises*, as it continues to allow its members to hold corporate directorships.[16]

Business leaders are often called upon to guide the policy-making process via advisory councils. As we documented, when the 2008 global financial crisis was in full meltdown, Finance Minister Jim Flaherty appointed an Economic Advisory Council composed purely of well-connected businesspeople. It met several times during preparation of the 2009 budget. In 2016, Finance Minister Bill Morneau followed suit. His fourteen-member Advisory Council on Economic Growth is extensively interlocked with corporate boards. In 2017, it released as its first report a proposal for an "infrastructure bank" that would be funded by the state, as a spur to corporate megaprojects.[17]

These examples point us to another kind of corporate reach into the state. "Regulatory capture," as James Kwak explains, is a "process by which regulation ... is consistently or repeatedly directed away from the public interest and toward the interests of the regulated industry by the intent and action of the industry itself." The most blatant examples involve "the fox guarding the henhouse," that is, the appointment of industry-friendly personnel to key state regulatory bodies. However, the influence process is often more subtle. Kwak goes on to analyze, as "cultural capture," the psycho-cultural mechanisms through which state regulators come to side with the industry they are supposed to be regulating. These include identifying with entrepreneurs as one's in-group, deferring to high-status people and gravitating toward positions advanced by those in one's social networks. The Alberta Energy Regulator (AER) and British

Columbia's Oil and Gas Commission are sterling examples of regulatory capture arising in part from their self-contradictory mandates to regulate the energy industry in the public interest while also promoting energy development. Both regulatory bodies are funded not by the state but by their respective industries, and AER's Chair, Gerry Protti, was formerly an executive in Encana, a major oil and gas producer/transporter. In Alberta, as James Wilt observes, it is much cheaper for a corporation to pay the relatively small fines that are occasionally assessed after major oil spills than to maintain safe pipelines. Moreover, the AER does not even have the resources to monitor spills or compliance. Journalist Andrew Nikiforuk has reported that a study by ecologist Kevin Timoney found the AER has vastly underestimated spill volumes and recovery efforts for decades. Such negligence not only allows corporations to externalize their costs, putting public safety and ecological health at risk. It paints a falsely reassuring picture of actual risks, at a time when scientists agree that a massive energy transition from carbon to renewable energy sources is urgently required.[18]

The federal regulatory body charged with overseeing the energy sector — the National Energy Board — provides another example of regulatory capture. In February 2017, a five-member panel assessed the NEB in response to a series of scandals. The panel reported that "Canadians have serious concerns that the NEB has been 'captured' by the oil and gas industry, with many Board members who come from the industry that the NEB regulates, and who — at the very least appear to — have an innate bias toward that industry." The panel recommended a complete overhaul, with appointments from a broad cross-section of society, a board of directors based not in Calgary but in Ottawa, and greater attention paid to Indigenous and environmental issues. In early 2018, the Trudeau Government announced that the NEB will be replaced by a new Canadian Energy Regulator. The demise of one captured regulator and the invention of a new regulator purports to address a number of the recommendations. At the time of writing, it remains to be seen whether the proposed legislation, which has yet to be adopted by Parliament, will enact a more democratic process or serve to re-legitimate an agency that has been thoroughly discredited.[19]

So far, we have emphasized the social and economic relations of corporate reach into civil and political society: elite interlocks, revolving doors, lobbying, regulatory capture, selective funding and the like. The allocative power of selective funding can also be seen in all manner of "astro-turf" groups: initiatives that have the veneer of grassroots organizations but are bankrolled by corporate capital. By diverting a small fraction of surplus value from accumulation, capital invests in populism. Such groups circumvent the obvious elitism of business councils yet they deliver similar messages to general publics and to a pro-business popular base. In the U.S., as science journalist Jeff Nesbit recounts, business activists like the Koch brothers (owners of the world's largest private oil company) have refined this surreptitious modus operandi into a science. The Kochs set up Citizens for a Sound Economy in 1984, running it effectively as a wholly owned subsidiary of Koch Industries until it morphed into Americans for Prosperity in 2004. That astro-turf group later gave rise to the Tea Party, also bankrolled by the Kochs and other capitalists. In Canada, corporate reach through astro-turfing has been less spectacular, and arguably less effective (after all, the Tea Party was a major force in the 2016 presidential election of Donald Trump). Still, groups like the CAPP-sponsored Canada's Energy Citizens play a role in mobilizing working-class people to support the status quo, typically out of fear that attempts to counter corporate power will imperil their jobs.[20]

DISCOURSES OF LEGITIMATION, MEDIA AND HEGEMONY

Complementing these social and economic relations are the "discourses of legitimation" that also reach into civil society, offering a steady stream of business-friendly perspectives. Such messaging emanates from many of the organizations we have considered above. Think tanks are constantly issuing reports, policy papers, media releases, info graphics, and more, to the media. Industry groups and business councils do the same, and all these organizations maintain information-rich websites.

But corporations themselves are key purveyors of pro-capitalist propaganda in two ways. On the one hand, companies producing retail products typically engage in extensive advertising, all of which normalizes and celebrates a way of life that equates commodity consumption with fulfilment. Where corporations seek to make controversial investments, such as oil and gas pipelines, they strive to win "social license" in the

Figure 6.3. Poster for CAPP's *"Energy Citizens" campaign*[21]

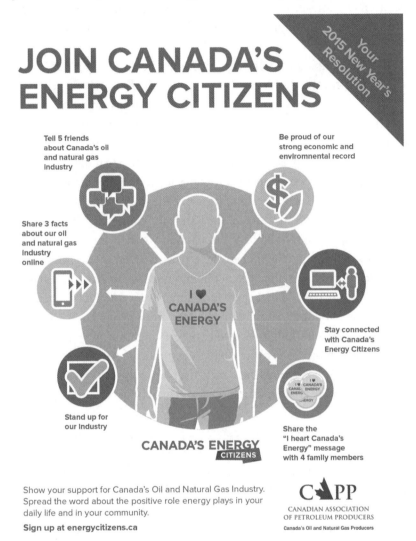

affected communities, using sophisticated public-relations techniques. In his "Mediatoil" project, communication researcher Patrick McCurdy has compiled a visual database of the various discourses of legitimation that the oil industry has pumped into civil society in the past decade, as well as competing discourses offered by Indigenous communities and social movements. The 2015 recruitment advertisement for CAPP's "Canada's Energy Citizens" exemplifies the corporate side in this discursive struggle. It invites each of us to show our love of "Canada's energy" by "standing up for our industry." In this imaginary, our interests and identities become indistinguishable from those of carbon capital. We are all "energy citizens."[22]

As this example shows, the battle for social licence to operate pipelines, and similar controversial, destructive practices, is part of a larger war for hearts and minds. Companies and industry groups intent on winning broad public support launch corporate social responsibility campaigns (CSR) to get the public onside. John Hilary, executive director of War on Want, argues that CSR is a corporate-driven initiative to remove or prevent state regulation. Such campaigns seek to substitute voluntary accords that enable "capital to set the terms of its own behaviour rather than succumb to external control." In Canada, the Trudeau regime has embraced CSR, particularly through its Ministry of Global Affairs, which now supports CSR abroad through its Office of the Extractive Sector Corporate Social Responsibility Counsellor. The neoliberal message in all CSR campaigns, as Hilary points out, is that there is no longer any conflict between business and society, and therefore no need for binding regulations and close oversight. Corporations may need some facilitation, but they "can be entrusted with the lead role in delivering public goods."[23]

On the other hand, mass media and the main players in social media are largely organized as a capitalist industry in which a few giant corporations dominate. The various genres of communication that media constantly pump into our living rooms and smart phones — news, entertainment, advertisements — fit within and reinforce a consumer-capitalist way of life, rather than raising challenges to that way of life. And as declining profit rates for mass-media corporations have decimated newsrooms, the remaining staff often rely on "information subsidies" to cut costs. These are provided for "free" by corporations (and state agencies) in the form of their own media releases, which are then relayed (sometimes verbatim) to viewers and readers. The corporate (and state) perspective is thereby marketed to the public as "news." As Kathleen Raso and Robert Neubauer surmise:

> Today a significant number — often a majority — of news stories are based on such "information subsidies." Unsurprisingly, information subsidization has been particularly prevalent in

contemporary pipeline politics, with the Alberta government having spent tens of millions of dollars annually to distribute pro-business messages through its Public Affairs bureau along with its more targeted pro-tar sands messaging campaigns.[24]

This is not to say that media discourse is all of one piece. Political economist David Model argues that there is considerable diversity in media content. But rarely do any corporate media challenge, or even call attention to, basic assumptions about the social and economic system:

> The point is to indoctrinate people continuously until neoliberal beliefs about the world become background assumptions. The advantage of background assumptions is that by their very nature they are not challenged, they are just assumed to be true. Such assumptions include materialism, consumerism, privatization, deregulation, the market system, and democracy in its present form. They are a major determining factor in what we are willing to believe about how our society functions.

Symbolic power is, as Robert Hackett and William Carroll have submitted, the power to represent, "to construct, define or name social reality, and thereby shape a very important component of the terrain on which all political struggles are conducted." This discursive power is magnified by the fact that just a few big companies dominate the field. The concentration of corporate revenue within giant media companies is also a "concentration of symbolic power in the means of public communication." According to Dwayne Winseck of the Canadian Media Concentration Research Project, the "big five" media corporations (Bell, Rogers, Telus, Shaw and Quebecor) account for nearly three-quarters of total revenue in the telecom/media/internet sector.[25]

As with other dimensions of corporate power, there is no backroom conspiracy behind this power to define the world and ourselves. Indeed, the profit motive that routinely steers life under capital plays an important role in corporate media power. As capitalist producers of culture, corporate media (whether television networks or Facebook) are in the business of selling audiences to advertisers. They make their profits from such sales. Canadian media theorist Dallas Smythe observed that the "main function of the mass media ... is to produce audiences prepared to be dutiful consumers." Social media take this process a step further, recruiting "prosumers" who consume while also producing their own online content, at no cost to the hosting corporation. In effect, as communications theorist Christian Fuchs notes, social-media corporations outsource work to unpaid prosumers:

> Javier Olivan, international manager at Facebook, commented that it would be cool to use the wisdom of the crowds. Pepsi started a competition, in which one could win US$ 10,000 for the best design of a Pepsi can. Ideabounty is a crowdsourcing platform that organizes crowdsourcing projects for corporations as for example RedBull, BMW or Unilever. In such projects, most of the employed work is unpaid. Even if single individuals receive symbolic prize money, most of the work time employed by users and consumers is fully unpaid, which allows companies to outsource paid labour time to consumers or fans that work for free.[26]

Perhaps most significantly of all, the power to legitimate capitalism is inscribed in the mundane technologies and social arrangements through which we live our lives. Two examples are networked information technologies (smart phones and personal computers) and automobility. Digital online communication, according to political scientist Jodi Dean, has "made capitalism acceptable, exciting and cool," while displacing critical energy into the work of personalizing one's online presence. In this way, the rise of corporate-owned social media "provided the basic components for neoliberalism's acceleration of capitalism, not to mention a bunch of super-fun diversions enabling people to feel radical and connected while playing on their laptops." As Dean writes:

> Enthusiastically participating in personal and social media—*I have broadband at home! My new tablet lets me work anywhere! With my smartphone I always know what's going on!*—we build the trap that captures us, a trap which extends beyond global use of mobile phones and participation in social networks to encompass the production of these phones and the hardware necessary to run these networks.[27]

But the penetration of corporate power into everyday life, shaping our identities and desires, is not exactly new. Geographer Matthew Huber has shown how, in post-war America, consumer capitalism was erected on the basis of a complex of oil-fuelled technologies and social arrangements: the automobile, the paved highway, suburbanization and widespread home ownership. Within this assemblage, the individual experiences automobility as empowering and liberating. The single detached house is a domain of personal sovereignty, or " property made possible through atomized entrepreneurial choices and individual energies." The long-range result has been to constrain politics within narrow limits "focused on the family, private property, and anticollectivst sentiments." This consumer-centred regime set the stage (as early as the 1970s) for middle-class tax revolt and the rise of neoliberalism. In postwar Canada, the same corporate hegemony developed around automobility and suburbanization, although arguably a social-democratic political current, grounded in a more robust labour movement, has tempered the tendency toward atomized individualism.[28]

WHEN HEGEMONY FAILS: HEIGHTENED SURVEILLANCE AND THE CRIMINALIZATION OF DISSENT

A final aspect of corporate reach into political society aligns corporations with the repressive arm of the state, as co-managers of dissent and surveillance. In Chapter 1 we emphasized that the state exercises a monopoly over the means of coercion — law, policing, taxation — and does so in the interests of protecting capitalist property. Although the ruling bloc prefers to govern with popular consent, when hegemony fails — when dissent becomes well organized and potentially effective — the state turns to more repressive strategies of social control. Three decades ago political scientist Andrew Gamble showed that neoliberalism's "free market" requires a "strong state" to protect capitalist interests from challenges from below, as market-driven politics place corporate interests above the public interest. Resistance to this corporate agenda arose initially in Canada in the 1980s and 1990s against the continental free trade deals. From the late 1990s onward, the opposition increasingly framed its project as more broadly anti-corporate, anti-austerity and anti-capitalist. There is much at stake in these struggles. Given the urgency of the climate crisis, it is not surprising that movements have mobilized great numbers of people to oppose, and even physically block, the various pipeline and infrastructure projects over the past decade. If built and used, this new energy infrastructure will inevitably push Canada's carbon footprint far beyond caps agreed to as part of the 2015 Paris climate accord.[29]

The state response has been to mobilize its security agencies (the RCMP and the Canadian Security Intelligence Service, CSIS) in collaboration with top fossil-fuel corporations, to protect "strategic infrastructure." Surveillance, the criminalization of dissent, the militarization of policing and the framing of "protestors, and political opposition in general, as a threat to economic recovery and competitiveness" have become the order of the day.[30]

An illuminating example comes from the federal Ministry of Public Safety, wherein Canada's Action Plan for Critical Infrastructure resides. Announced in 2010 and launched at a 2012 summit co-hosted by the Canadian Gas Association and the Canadian Energy Pipeline Association, the project to strengthen "the resilience of Canada's critical infrastructure" brings together the RCMP and CSIS as partners to other federal and provincial agencies and critical infrastructure "owners/operators." A 2014 RCMP intelligence report leaked by Greenpeace warns of "violent anti-petroleum extremists" driven by an "anti-petroleum ideology," and exemplifies where this criminalization of dissent leads. Investigative journalist Carol Linnitt recounts that the confidential report was prepared for critical infrastructure "stakeholders" such as pipeline companies, who play increasingly collaborative roles with the state in protecting their investments. Under Bill C-51, passed by the Harper Government in 2015, these stakeholders were granted special security clearance, while those who interfere with such infrastructure or with the economic and financial stability of Canada were tagged as terrorists. Bill C-59, introduced by the Trudeau Government in the summer of 2017, softened the language a little (and increased state powers of surveillance). But the Bill continued to target "interference with critical infrastructure" as a threat to national security and to allow authorities to detain protestors by "preventative arrest," as Elizabeth Rowley has noted.[31]

Public Safety Canada's website describes the new National Strategy as one of close partnership between state and corporate business:

> Critical infrastructure owners and operators have the expertise and information that governments need to develop comprehensive emergency management plans. In turn, governments will share relevant information in a timely manner, respecting existing federal, provincial and territorial legislation and policies, to help owners and operators assess risk and identify best practices. This partnership approach recognizes that more resilient critical infrastructure helps foster an environment that stimulates economic growth, attracts and retains business, and creates employment opportunities.... The National Strategy establishes a framework for cooperation in which governments and owners and operators can work together to prevent, mitigate, prepare for, respond to, and recover from disruptions of critical infrastructure and thereby safeguard the foundations of our country and way of life.

As opposition to the expansion of fossil-fuel infrastructure threatens the smooth functioning of the commodity chain, the state's coercive arm becomes more immediately engaged in protecting the "rights" of corporations, and it does so in close partnership with those corporations. Mi'kmaq activist Barbara Low (quoted by Bruce Livesey) concludes: "the Canadian government is working specifically for the oil and gas industry. It is completely intertwined."[32]

Chapter 7

BEYOND CORPORATE OLIGARCHY
Resistance and Alternatives

This book has charted the many modalities of corporate power that have shaped and continue to shape Canada as a settler-capitalist society. In this chapter, we focus on the social forces of counter-power, and the alternative policies and visions these forces are putting forward today.

There are, in fact, long and strong traditions of resistance to corporate power in Canada. For many years, Indigenous resistance has focused on maintaining traditional collectivist and sustainable ways of life and ways of knowing. Recently, this resistance has blossomed into a resurgent politics of decolonization, which many non-Indigenous Canadians are beginning to support. Alliances between Indigenous campaigners, environmentalists and others, forged in struggles at flashpoints arrayed along carbon commodity chains, exemplify this encouraging development. "Analytically," as Elaine Coburn and Clifford Atleo emphasize, "resurgence encompasses resistance, since the critical reinvention of Indigenous principles and practices resists assimilationist and integrationist colonial-capitalist logics and relationships." Indigenous resurgence, with its insistence on reviving and continuing to advance community-based ways of life, which precede capitalism by many centuries, is a strong current in the contemporary search for viable post-capitalist alternatives. This is not to deny the reach of neoliberal capitalism into Indigenous communities. Indeed, some Indigenous leaders did join a project of Aboriginal economic development that, as Coburn and Atleo note, "celebrates individualism, entrepreneurship and the generation of profits, subsuming concerns for the environment" while urging "integration into a despiritualized world understood simply as a business opportunity." As with other strands of counter-power, Indigenous resistance/resurgence must continually struggle against its own cooptation into corporate-capitalist projects.[1]

Much the same can be said of the labour movement, whose roots in Canada reach back to the nineteenth century. Many of the measures that enable employees to live decent lives — the eight hour day, legally enforced employment standards, paid vacations, pensions, Medicare and so on — are accomplishments of the labour movement and aligned political parties, particularly the New Democratic Party. None of these measures were ever given away by capital and the state. Yet, particularly in the "golden era" of postwar capitalism (roughly 1945–1975), the reform agenda to give capitalism a human face led organized labour into a class compromise that weakened the movement's capacity to struggle for a better world beyond capital. Instead, the goal was to claim a greater share of the wealth produced by labour, so that workers could afford more of the burgeoning volume of commodities produced within consumer capitalism. But the logic of this approach ties labour ever more tightly to the accumulation needs of capital, which include (as we emphasized in Chapter 1) a dangerously growing carbon footprint, among other ecological maladies.

This brings us to the question of left and right. As historian Ian McKay notes, "We live in an intensely right-wing era." The lustre of the postwar boom is long past. We now cling to the wreckage. Most employees have, for many years, coped with stagnating or even falling real wages, as rates of unionization have declined (from 37.9 percent in 1984 to 28.4 in 2016, according to Statistics Canada). Taking inflation into account, journalist Amy Minsky reports that since the 1970s "the minimum wage and the average hourly wage are essentially unchanged." In a world of deepening ecological crisis and a failed neoliberal political paradigm, is the much-hyped notion, championed by the federal Liberal government, to "grow the middle class" a project of the left? Is the labour movement a conduit for that project?[2]

Ian McKay's thinking can be helpful here. As he recounts, "left and right" have their origins in the French Revolution, when those that wanted to abolish the King's veto power over the democratically elected parliament sat to the left of the President. The left has always pushed for more, deeper and radical, democracy. Democracy, in fact, "belongs to the left." When it comes to discerning who is on the left, today, McKay opines:

> Anybody who shares four key insights — that is, into capitalism's injustice, the possibility of equitable democratic alternatives, the need for social transformation, and the real-world development of the preconditions of this social transformation in the actual world around us — can be called a leftist.

The left is about much more than "growing the middle class." The left seeks a world beyond the capital/labour relation that is foundational to corporate power. Creating democratic alternatives that challenge, roll back and extinguish that power also goes well beyond narrowly framed trade union agendas for higher pay, although unions have been and will continue to be key centres of workplace activism in the democratic impulse that is at the heart of the left.[3] Moreover, although opposition to capitalism's injustices is integral to the left, all emancipatory social movements have at least a foot in the left (and vice versa). Capitalism as a way of life intersects with and reinforces gendered, racialized and other inequities while posing the greatest barrier to recuperating the health of the Earth. In the struggle against corporate plutocracy, there is much common ground in the converging agendas of feminist, anti-racist, environmental and other critical social movements.

The contradiction between McKay's definition of the left and the logic of corporate capital is profound. As we saw in earlier chapters, the property and power relations at the core of corporate capital are fundamentally anti-democratic. They give major corporate shareholders voting power according to how much capital is owned, and they disenfranchise the rest of us. In this book we have analyzed the various modalities of corporate power: the operational power of management, the strategic control of corporations, the allocative power of finance, the social power of the corporate elite as a tiny, organized minority and the political and cultural reach of corporate capital into state and civil society. All of these operate on the basis of an anti-democratic logic that empowers and rewards those who own and control capital. Corporate power is power-over: over workers, over finance and investment (and thus the future), over communities and governments, over the marginalized and dispossessed, and over ecosystems, which get reduced to "natural resources" to be extracted at the lowest cost. However, power-over is just one form of power in human relations. To repeat a point we borrowed from Lisa Veneklasen and Valerie Miller, "power-to" is the exercise of one's own agency in shaping one's world and one's self in it. "Power-with" develops as people gain collective strength through collaboration with peers, based on mutual support.[4]

We begin our discussion of alternatives to corporate power by recalling that these alternative forms — power-with and power-to — hold the keys to getting past the logic of corporate capital. When the left calls for democracy, when Indigenous activists call for resurgence, it is these forms of power that are at stake. Political theorist Robert Albritton's conception of "human flourishing" as the centrepiece of alternatives to capitalism's power-over is useful here. Defining human flourishing as "what we know about how to make our lives more fulfilling while improving the health of the earth for future generations," Albritton makes two important suggestions. First, as an overall vision or goal, "social life should aim to maximize the human flourishing of each, consistent with the human flourishing of all." Second, although this ethical vision will take generations to realize in any comprehensive way, "it is a utopia worth working towards, by always working to remove those barriers that seem most damaging to human flourishing in the present." This conception of flourishing combines power-to and power-with, pointing toward a democratic way of life. For us, it raises the question, how can we resist corporate power-over while removing the barriers it poses to our shaping the world, in collaboration with peers, and in the direction of greater flourishing?[5]

If we use this lens to reconsider each modality of corporate power, the alternative that comes into focus is a project of economic democratization, from the workplace to the furthest reaches of financialized capital accumulation. As we reconsider each modality of corporate power, we highlight, on one hand, the interventions that can erode that power and the alternatives that can replace it.

ERODING AND REPLACING CORPORATIONS' ECONOMIC POWER

At its most concrete level, corporate power is founded on a relationship of exploitation between capital and labour. The economic surplus that labour creates is appropriated as capitalist profit (and further divided into streams of interest for banks and rent for landowners). Within the corporation, operational power reaches down from the executive suite to the shop floor, to maximize the amount of surplus value taken by capital. For many, work is an experience of alienation, a deduction from life. It is time spent under the control of bosses, earning the wages that fund a life apart from the workplace. To democratize the workplace means shifting from the hierarchical structures of contemporary corporate management to arrangements that enable workers to be creative agents, in control of their labour (power-to) while collaborating with co-workers on an egalitarian basis (power-with). Unions, of course, are a countervailing and democratizing power in the workplace. Their collective agreements with employers are subject to democratic vote by members and contain a range of clauses limiting the arbitrary power of managers and enabling workers to make grievances against unjust treatment. Public policy can also play an important role in curtailing management's power, through establishing and enforcing employment standards to protect workers' health, safety and human rights. Such interventions erode the corporate capital's operational power, but they do not offer an alternative to the basic structure of top-down management.

There is, however, a long history of workplace democracy, originating in early nineteenth century critiques of capitalism, which has been spearheaded by worker cooperatives. Cooperatives are collectively owned enterprises that are democratically controlled by their members, for their mutual benefit. Management is elected by the members on the basis of one member, one vote. In place of the many-tiered, strict hierarchy of corporate management, cooperatives emphasize worker participation in decision-making, that is, self-management through councils composed of workers. Globally, the cooperative sector is large and growing. As researcher and activist John Restakis notes:

> With over 800 million members in 85 countries the co-operative movement is by far the most durable and most powerful grass-roots movement in the world. Co-operatives employ more people in democratically run enterprises than all the world's multinational corporations combined.

Restakis goes on to explain "the restorative power of co-operation", its capacity to promote human thriving in place of alienation and precarity.

Whereas corporations treat workers as a means toward private profit:

> Co-operatives invite worker-members to invest their identities in their work, to see their work as extensions of themselves through the mechanisms of shared ownership and personal control. Any workplace can undergo a profound change in meaning if it shifts from being primarily a vehicle for the generation of profit over which one has no control, to being a community of relationships with an inherent worth of its own. This is perhaps the quintessential difference between the co-operative and the capitalist firm. In one, the enterprise is a means to the human fulfillment of all through the creation of community. In the other, the enterprise is a means to the fulfillment of some through the subordination of others.[6]

Although many cooperatives operate on a small scale, in Spain the Mondragon complex of interlinked cooperatives, founded in 1956, employs 75,000 worker-members across a range of industrial, financial and commercial sectors. Its success demonstrates that the cooperative model can be effectively scaled up, as the contributions of individual cooperatives to the Mondragon Cooperative Corporation "strengthen the system's infrastructure, which not only aims at preserving the cooperative organization, but also expanding it", according to political economist Chris Rogers.[7]

Mondragon also offers a lesson in how democratizing an enterprise leads to other socially just outcomes. Cooperatives, through democratic ownership and control, can mitigate the divide between top earners and the rest of us. At Mondragon, worker-members have long placed a cap on pay differentials between top and bottom earners. Currently, as James Rowe and his colleagues report, the highest paid member-worker earns no more than 6 times the pay of the lowest paid member-worker. In Canada, top CEOs currently earn 209 times an average worker's salary. Rowe and his co-authors emphasize that public policy can be torqued to encourage the development of cooperatives. In Spain, for instance, cooperatives are taxed at a lower rate than corporations. The burgeoning cooperative sector in Quebec has benefited from provincially-funded Regional Development Cooperatives, with the mandate to support creation of new cooperatives while strengthening existing ones.[8]

In Chapter 3 we described how the corporate quest for maximal profit has restructured the workplace, introducing bureaucratic and other forms of labour control that limit workers' creative agency and collaboration. The legacy left by corporate reorganization is that a majority of jobs entail relatively undesirable and disempowering tasks, whereas the minority (most of them managerial and professional) entail mostly desirable and empowering tasks. As advocates of the Participatory Economics (ParEcon) model point out:

> The uneven distribution of tasks in hierarchical economies makes the labour and life of some more empowering and often more desirable than the labour of others. Additionally, this minority tend to monopolise information and knowledge at the workplace because they do most of the empowering tasks. Since influence over economic decision-making is affected by the knowledge obtained at the workplace, it is likely that those workers who obtain more confidence and knowledge will dominate meetings and discussions even when each worker has one vote.

Even in cooperative workplaces, residues of this legacy need to be eroded through conscious interventions. One approach, championed by ParEcon, is the creation of "balanced jobs." Workers' councils are tasked with re-composing jobs so that each one affords opportunities for creative agency and collaboration. Such balancing of the burdens and benefits of labour promotes the values of self-management and equity while eroding the hierarchy of operational power, including the division between the managed and the managers. As cooperative organization, job balancing and related alternatives to business-as-usual workplaces take root, broader cultural changes become feasible. In civil society, values of solidarity and equity gain strength, undercutting the possessive individualism that underwrites neoliberal capitalism.[9]

Democratizing the workplace through self-management is not only a viable alternative to corporate organization of the private sector. Public enterprises and government departments can also be democratized in this way, creating platforms for democratic rather than bureaucratic planning., As political scientist Greg Albo suggests:

> Self-management should also be extended upwards to sectoral

national planning councils, where sustainable production might actually be negotiated and realized. In addition, workplace democracy has a role to play within government departments in terms of extension of workplace rights, and in the election by public-sector workers of managers and representatives for departmental and sectoral councils.[10]

As we saw in Chapter 4, the strategic power to determine who sits on a corporation's board of directors concentrates corporate power among a small number of big shareholders, both individual and institutional. This modality of corporate power is strongly entrenched, yet there is nothing "natural" about it, and it is not beyond the reach of progressive reform.

How can the control of enterprises be democratized? Perhaps the most immediate intervention that erodes power is shareholder activism. Activist shareholders use their ownership stake to put pressure on corporate management. In many cases the goal is simply to grab more of the economic surplus for themselves, rather than seeing it go to overstuffed CEOs. More interestingly, some forms of shareholder activism embrace social justice and ecological values. An example is Vancouver-based Shareholder Association for Research and Education (SHARE). SHARE works with institutional investors to implement "responsible investment strategies and to amplify their voices in support of a sustainable economy." SHARE also engages state managers and regulators to increase the transparency and accountability of corporations regarding a range of ecological and social issues. Guided by a directorate composed primarily of labour leaders, SHARE helps organize socially and environmentally responsible institutional investors to pressure corporations on issues that include climate change and "decent work." Pressure may take the form of voting as a bloc at the corporation's annual general meeting, or insisting on greater attention by corporate boards to issues such as "stranded assets," a looming threat that Canadian fossil-fuel firms tend to downplay. Research by Carbon Tracker has shown that, to meet its commitment to the 2015 Paris Climate accord, Canada will have to keep most of its carbon assets in the ground, stranding them from capitalist extraction. Yet corporations continue to claim them as burnable reserves. A recent SHARE investigation found that only 28 percent of energy companies listed on the Toronto Stock Exchange acknowledge the risk of stranded assets to their shareholders.[11]

More direct approaches to economic democratization at the level of corporate governance have been pursued in Europe. The German system of "co-determination" is one instance. Since 1976, large employers have been required by the German state to allow workers to elect just under half of members of their supervisory boards, with the other half elected by investors on the basis of shares owned. As Tom Malleson notes, such shared corporate governance (which also exists in five other European countries) gives workers a direct say in corporate strategy.[12]

More ambitious still was the Meidner plan, which marked the high tide of Swedish social democracy. In 1976, Rudolph Meidner, chief economist at Sweden's largest trade union federation, introduced a plan for a share levy on corporations with more than fifty employees. Companies would be obliged to issue new shares each year, equal to 20 percent of their profits. The new shares could not be sold, but would be given to a network of "wage earner funds," representing workers and local authorities. Robin Blackburn explains the logic of this plan: local authorities would reinvest income from dividends to finance future social expenditure, and "as the wage earner funds grew they would be able to play an increasing part in directing policy in the corporations they owned." Indeed, within a couple of decades or so, the majority shareholders in all Swedish corporations would be the wage earner funds, The plan was brilliant as it transferred strategic control of corporations from the capitalist class to labour and local governments. The transfer mechanism was not wholesale nationalization (which is very expensive), and it did not involve taxing corporate profits (which causes a drag on business). Instead, by gradually diluting private capitalist ownership and enlarging ownership by workers and communities, capitalists' strategic power-over could be removed, without dispossessing them from their investments. Meidner's plan, however, was opposed by the moderate leadership of Sweden's Labour Party, who were committed to building the welfare state, not transcending capitalism. Ultimately, in response to what Meidner called "the tumultuous campaigns" by the capitalist class and its allies "to fend off 'socialist aggression,'" the Meidner plan was watered down to a mild package of reforms that could not erode the power of capitalist owners. Although the Meidner plan was ultimately the road not taken, given political will, it illustrates how an incremental approach to shifting strategic control of corporations from capitalists to workers and communities is feasible.[13]

What, then, of the third modality of economic power: the allocative power of finance? The classic call of the left in this respect has been for the socialization of banks, bringing them under democratic control through public ownership. The forerunner to the NDP, the Co-operative Commonwealth Federation, featured this demand in its founding Regina Manifesto. More recently, during the global financial meltdown of 2008, when governments were busy directing vast sums to troubled financial institutions (to be later paid for by cutbacks to social programs), political scientist Leo Panitch made the reasonable suggestion that banks should be operated as public utilities, as a service delivered in the public interest rather than the interests of the corporate oligarchy. Similarly, Richard Swift has argued that "only by making finance a public service will we gain the chance to redesign it to serve society's goals of distributional fairness and ecological sanity." This position also implies public ownership. As with Swedish wage earner funds, such an initiative poses a direct challenge to corporate power, which means that the option is really only available to a strong, united left that enjoys broad public support. Technically, however, the socialization of Canada's banks is entirely feasible. Economist David Macdonald has calculated that in the wake of the 2008 meltdown, it would have been less expensive for the federal government to bring banks like the Canadian Imperial Bank of Commerce under public ownership than to bail them out.[14]

Again, however, public ownership is not sufficient. After all, Canada's public pension funds — the Canada Pension Plan and the Quebec Pension Plan — are run exactly like a corporation, by corporate players and advisors, with the blind objective of profit maximization. To democratize finance means democratizing the governance of such institutions while mandating them to support socially and ecologically healthy investment. Here, shifting from power-over to power-to and power-with requires a move to "participatory planning." Such democratic planning replaces the capitalist standpoint (planning focused purely on profit) with what Marx once called the standpoint of "social humanity." It also changes who is at the table, replacing capitalists and technocrats with voices representing "social humanity." As Marta Harnecker has commented, "It is only through such a process that society can truly appropriate the fruits of its labor."[15]

Participatory budgeting which was introduced in the Brazilian city of Porto Alegre in 1989, presents one example of how the process works:

> Participatory budgeting has developed into an annual process of deliberation and decision-making, in which thousands of city residents decide how to allocate part of the municipal budget. In a series of neighbourhood, regional, and citywide assemblies, residents and elected budget delegates identify spending priorities and vote on which priorities to implement.

As the Transnational Institute concludes from its study of participatory budgeting in Canada:

> while changing spending policies, participatory budgeting also transforms the way these policies are decided. It thus moves us closer to a more democratic and participatory political system, and helps participants learn to act more democratically. Participatory budgeting in Canada has only affected small segments of local governance so far, but the initial experiences reveal new ways to broaden and deepen democratic participation.[16]

A challenge, then, is how to scale up participatory budgeting and how to apply it in the allocation of society's resources. One initiative worth noting is the Canadian Centre for Policy Alternative's "Alternative Federal Budget," an annual "what if" exercise that brings knowledgeable citizens together to show "what a government could do if it were truly committed to an economic, social, and environmental agenda that reflects the values of the large majority of Canadians — as opposed to the interests of a privileged few."[17]

Bringing centres of allocative power under democratic control is obviously a tall order and not on the immediate horizon. But interventions that can begin to erode that power include the Tobin Tax. First suggested by Nobel laureate economist James Tobin in 1972, the tax would be levied at a low rate of perhaps 0.5 percent on all financial transactions that involve currency exchange (for example, trading dollars for yen). This relatively simple measure would dampen speculative capital flows across national borders. Slowing down cross-border speculation in this way would help erode the structural power of capital and rein in the global casino economy that has flourished since neoliberal deregulation in the 1980s. Tobin himself held that "a reasonable estimate of the amount to be derived from the Tobin Tax would be as much as half trillion dollars a year, give or take a couple hundred billions," which could be put to public use. However, as labour researcher Thomas Palley pointed out, "over time financial markets will undoubtedly innovate in directions that evade a Tobin tax — as it might be imagined today." More recently, Robert Pollin and his colleagues at the Political Economy Research Institute have proposed, as an extension of the Tobin Tax, a securities transaction tax that would apply to all transactions involving securities, pre-empting investors from tax avoidance.[18]

In our select review of alternatives, a final intervention to erode corporate capital's allocative power is exemplified by the divestment movement. Divestment is the opposite of investment: it removes funding from activities considered unethical. When divestment is politically organized it can pose a counter-power to (amoral) business-as-usual. As the activist website Fossil Free recalls, the most impactful divestment campaign to date focused on South African Apartheid, which corporate capital was all too happy to support, until a grassroots movement intervened:

> By the mid-1980s, 155 [U.S.] campuses — including some of the most famous in the country — had divested from companies doing business in South Africa. 26 state governments, 22 counties, and 90 cities, including some of the nation's biggest, took their money from multinationals that did business in the country. The South African divestment campaign helped break the back of the Apartheid government and usher in an era of democracy and equality.

Today, the fossil fuel divestment campaign is "the fastest growing corporate campaign of its kind in history," according to Desmond Tutu, a leader of the struggle against Apartheid. Political scientist James Rowe and his colleagues hold that fossil fuel divestment targets the concentrated economic power of carbon capital and the ways that power has been mobilized to obstruct decarbonization and democratization. They describe divestment as "a crucial step in not only the needed energy transition, but also the transition to a genuinely sustainable economic system." As divestment campaigns develop, activists learn that the financial enablers of carbon capitalism are just as complicit as the producing companies, "with the financial industry intricately linked to the financing, insurance and speculative interests of the oil and gas sector," according to Greg Albo and Lilian Yap.[19]

This is a lesson with radical implications, even if, as Jordan Kinder argues, divestment alone "does not (and *will* not) significantly disrupt the totalizing forces of fossil capital." Circling back to a modality of corporate power we discussed in Chapter 3, Kinder points out that blockades along carbon-capital commodity chains, often led by Indigenous activists, can also be effective in disrupting and delaying the smooth functioning of those chains while affirming Indigenous resurgence. Kinder concludes that aspects of divestment and blockade can be brought together into a broader "counter-hegemonic" strategy that goes beyond resistance:

> From divestment we can take its non-locality and from blockade we can take its tendency towards locality, its method of targeting unjust infrastructures, and, most importantly, its negation-affirmation. Coordinated efforts are absolutely essential as neither divestment nor blockade alone can build a politics on the scale necessary to dismantle fossil capital.

Indeed, the various interventions and alternatives we review in this chapter are complementary and need to be taken up in combination.[20]

ERODING AND REPLACING CORPORATIONS' HEGEMONIC POWER

Deepening democracy in the socio-cultural and political fields means eroding and eliminating the *reach* of corporate power — in particular the role of big money (capital's allocative power) in politics and culture, as well as the inordinately strong voice corporate capital projects in these domains. Big money and corporate voice distort the conversations that are integral to a democratic way of life. As feminist political theorist Nancy Fraser has argued, such a way of life requires that all parties to a decision-making process participate on a level playing field and that there is "parity of participation." A robust, participatory democracy is a far cry from the hollowed-out, neoliberal democracy that Canada has become in the past few decades as a result of implementing the corporate agenda. As

Jordan Kinder implies, not only must corporate power be eroded, it must be replaced with people's power. This means building a broad counter-hegemonic strategy that brings together the various critical movements — Indigenous, feminist, labour, environmentalist — that are striving for a world beyond corporate power.[21]

Space only allows us to gesture toward the kinds of changes that can erode corporate hegemony while fostering parity of participation. Here are three very basic reforms, targeted at political society:

- Big money must be removed from the political process. Reforms to election financing (including third-party campaigns sponsored by corporate players) are an obvious step. Quebec's recently adopted regulations, banning corporate donations and limiting individual donations to $100, are a good model for the rest of Canada.
- Similarly, corporate access to government through lobbying needs to be monitored and limited. A recent study by SHARE found many deficiencies in the various "lobbyist registries" that are intended to provide disclosure of corporate contacts with public office hold-ers. Contrary to current practice, authors Brittany Stares and Kevin Thomas recommended that "companies can and should report broadly on the policy activity they undertake, as well as any mem-berships in and contributions to outside organizations (e.g. trade associations, think tanks, etc.)." Greater transparency of this sort, while a small step, is important. Equally important as a modest reform is the elimination of "revolving doors" through which public office holders move seamlessly into the corporate sector as lobby-ists, bringing with them their knowledge and contacts, and thereby enhancing corporate influence.[22]
- Corporate capture of regulatory bodies like the National Energy Board needs to be unwound, and corporate representation on the boards of public bodies (including crown corporations like the CBC) should be strictly limited. As a general rule of thumb, public bodies (including universities) should be governed by informed citizens and community leaders who have the public interest at heart.

On a wider scale, economic democratization also means re-negotiating the various international agreements that provide much of the archi-tecture of transnational neoliberalism, transforming them from "free trade" and investors' rights agreements like NAFTA to fair trade, with strong social and environmental clauses. For more than three decades, the Council of Canadians has led the grassroots struggle against these arrangements. As Jerry Diaz (president of Unifor, Canada's largest industrial union) and Council of Canadians Chairperson Maude Barlow have stated:

> NAFTA captures the worst features of corporate-led, profit-driven globalization, providing transnational businesses unconditional access to markets with no requirement to invest where they sell and the right to scour a continent in search of the cheapest labour, weakest regulations and biggest tax breaks. With its remarkably poor, and unenforceable, labour provisions, NAFTA hangs like a spectre over the heads of industrial workers, the persistent threat of job loss used to justify cuts to wages and benefits.

Neoliberalism's corporate agenda, institutionalized in deals like NAFTA, needs to give way to a political agenda of social justice.[23]

To address the ongoing injustice of colonization, this agenda must include full implementation of United Nations Declaration on the Rights of Indigenous Peoples (UNDRIP). Passed in September 2007 with 144 states in favour (and Canada, the US, Australia and New Zealand opposed), UNDRIP "establishes a universal framework of minimum standards for the survival, dignity and well-being of the indigenous peoples of the world." A decade later, in September 2017, British Columbia became the first Canadian government to declare that it will be henceforth governed by UNDRIP. As policy researcher Rosie Simms and her colleagues note, respecting UNDRIP means breaking with unilateral colonial arrangements in favour of "collaborative consent" and "embracing the critical role of Indigenous nations as full partners in building Canada's future."[24]

As we saw in Chapter 6, corporate reach into civil society is extensive. It shapes the way we think about our world and ourselves. To democratize civil society means building the capacity of non-profit, community-based organizations across a range of fields. This includes the policy-planning process, currently dominated by corporate-funded think tanks closely tied to the corporate elite. Fortunately, Canada has a number of social justice–oriented policy institutes, such as the Canadian Centre for Policy Alternatives, Parkland Institute, Broadbent Institute and Institut de recherche et d'informations socioéconomiques. These need to be fostered and heard, as centres for innovative policy alternatives which often draw upon participatory approaches.[25]

Corporate domination of cultural life raises especially big challenges. Pro-business discourses of legitimation reach into civil society, persuading us to identify our needs with corporate interests. Corporate power works both *through* the media (as conduits for pro-business messaging) and *over* the media (which, as profit-maximizing corporations, prioritize commerce above civic goals such as fostering an informed citizenry). Key to eroding, and replacing, capital's symbolic power through and over media is a vibrant movement to democratize media, which is so far in a nascent state. A full-scale media democratization project could transform/ reform the corporate media system while also transforming the lifeworld through independent media, media education and an enlarged "digital commons," which Guy Aitchison defines as "a space free from the rule of private property and the state." It would, as Bob Hackett and William Carroll have claimed, "pose challenges to hegemony in everyday culture (delegitimizing corporate media, building democratic alternatives, etc.) but also in the long march through the institutions." The latter includes, among other reforms, strengthening public-interest media, such as the CBC/Radio Canada, and protecting net neutrality against corporate enclosure.[26]

TOWARD AN AUTHENTIC DEMOCRACY

Threaded together, these various measures to erode and replace corporate power comprise a line of transitional reforms opening toward a more democratic way of life. However, no one measure is a magic key. Economic democratization needs to proceed on all fronts. The core set of reforms would replace the economic power of the corporate elite with a "solidarity economy." Such an economy, as sociologist Michelle Williams argues, "seeks to overcome capitalism through a democratic pluralist process of worker and popular control of the means of production, distribution and consumption." There is no blueprint for this "but rather a continual process of (re)making social relations based on democratic practices, local bottom-up experiments, redistribution, solidarity, interconnections, reciprocity and social justice." The core operating principle of corporate capitalism — endless accumulation based on the alienation and exploitation of labour and an extractive relationship to the rest of nature — would give way to a principle of reciprocity. Reciprocity, John Restakis reminds us, "is the social mechanism that makes associational life possible." Restakis writes, "As opposed to the capitalist principle of capital control over labour, reciprocity is the means by which a social interest — whether labor, citizen groups or consumers — can exercise control over capital."[27]

Looming over this scenario for transitioning from a Canada ruled by corporate power to a genuine democracy is the ecological crisis. Within that crisis the danger of catastrophic climate change grows with every uptick in capital accumulation. As political ecologists Christopher Wright and Daniel Nyberg have stated:

> Economic growth and the exploitation of nature have long gone hand-in-hand, but they now constitute the most ill-fated of bedfellows. Climate change, the greatest threat of our time, is the definitive manifestation of the well-worn links between progress and devastation. And as we continue to shamble towards a tipping point from which any meaningful return will be utterly impossible, a familiar message rings out from the corporate world: "business as usual."[28]

As historian Andreas Malm has shown, the accumulation of fossil capital is the driving force in climate change. Eroding and transforming corporate power in and around this sector is an urgent task for movements and progressive governments. The scientific consensus holds that in order to avoid catastrophic climate change the world will have to de-carbonize energy in the next three decades. By implication, most of the world's carbon (especially the dirtiest deposits) must remain in the ground. Robust regulatory practices, including full-cost accounting that prevents companies from externalizing costs, are means of eroding fossil capital's power. But what is required is a deeper, just transition. Power must shift in a double sense. As power-over is transformed into power-to and power-with through democratizing the economy (and state), the energy that powers our machines, households and communities must also shift from fossil fuels to clean energy. The combination of these shifts from fossil-fuelled power to renewables (de-carbonization) and from corporate plutocracy to public, democratic control of economic decisions (democratization) is now called "energy democracy." Endorsed by the international trade union movement, including Canada's largest unions and the Canadian Labour Congress, energy democracy offers an appealing alternative to continued corporate rule and eventual ecocide.[29]

Braided together, these threads offer a lifeline to what Fred Magdoff and John Bellamy Foster have called "sustainable human development." In mainstream discourse, "development" is code for capital accumulation. What gets "developed" are markets, financial empires, transnational corporations and commodity chains, extreme inequities and ecological overshoot. Human beings and ecosystems are simply means toward accumulation, or collateral damage. In place of an unsustainable "development" that amplifies corporate power, Canada and the wider world need a new paradigm centred not on capital accumulation but on human flourishing within a thriving ecosystem. The Indigenous concept of *buen vivir* — living well, not having more — is central to this social vision. In place of the treadmill of production — the frenetic accumulation of things as we foul our own nest — *buen vivir* points us to the enrichment of our social relations and cultural life as daily life is slowed down, allowing us "to maximise time for free activities conducted in a stable and well-maintained environment," according to geographer David Harvey.[30]

To make such an alternative real will require concerted collective action, popular participation and social learning from below. Building a strong, united, democratic left and a broad culture of solidarity and social justice is what enables real challenges to corporate power. In the process, not only do we change our circumstances, we change ourselves, thereby creating capacities for authentic self-governance. As political economist Michael Lebowitz has written, "Practice, collective action, struggle of the people to rule the commons — these are the ways to build the rule of the people; this is the protagonistic democracy by which both circumstances and people are transformed." Only on that basis can corporate power be placed where it actually belongs: in the dustbin of history.[31]

NOTES

Chapter 1 Notes

1. <https://en.wikipedia.org/wiki/Financial_District,_Toronto> accessed 6 March 2018.
2. Azeezah Kanji, "Imagine cities that shelter people, not war," Toronto *Star*, 11 January 2018 <https://www.thestar.com/opinion/contributors/2018/01/11/imagine-cities-that-shelter-people-not-war.html> accessed 6 March, 2018. "Nearly 100 homeless people died in Toronto in 2017," CBC News 29 January 2018 <http://www.cbc.ca/news/canada/toronto/homeless-deaths-toronto-public-health-1.4509218> accessed 6 March 2018. "Record-breaking CEO pay now 209 times more than average worker," Canadian Centre for Policy Alternatives, 2 January 2018 <https://www.policyalternatives.ca/newsroom/news-releases/record-breaking-ceo-pay-now-209-times-more-average-worker> accessed 6 March 2018.
3. Karl Marx, *Capital: A Critique of Political Economy, Vol. 1*, translated by Samuel Moore and Edward Aveling, 1887 [1867] <https://www.marxists.org/archive/marx/works/1867-c1/ch33.htm> accessed 24 July 2017, quote from Chapter 33, paragraph 1. Michael A. Lebowitz, *Beyond Capital*, London: Macmillan, 1992.
4. Peter Blau, *Exchange and Power in Social Life*, New York: John Wiley, 1964.
5. Ibid., Chapter 6, paragraph 19. In the quote, "Bentham" refers to Jeremy Bentham, a British utilitarian philosopher who viewed free-market capitalism as providing the greatest happiness for the greatest number.
6. Gerald Horne, *The Counter-Revolution of 1776*, New York: New York University Press, 2014.
7. Karl Marx, *Capital*, Chapter 33, paragraph 1.
8. Alfredo Saad-Filho, "Value, capital and exploitation," in Alfredo Saad-Filho (ed.), *Anti-Capitalism*, London: Pluto Press, 2003: 27–40.
9. Jim Stanford, *Economics for Everyone*, Halifax: Fernwood Publishing, 2008: 71.
10. Source of data: Statistics Canada. Table 380-0076 Current and capital accounts – Corporations, annual (accessed 17 September 2017).
11. Leo A. Johnson, 1977, *Poverty in Wealth: The Capitalist Labour Market and Income Distribution in Canada*, Toronto: New Hogtown Press.
12. Ben Fine, *Marx's Capital*, London: Macmillan, 1984: 36.

13. William K. Carroll, *Corporate Power in a Globalizing World*, Don Mills: Oxford University Press, 2004: 3. Saad-Filho, "Value, capital and exploitation."

14. James O'Connor, *Natural Causes*, New York: Guilford Press, 1998.

15. Philip Cross and Philippe Bergevin, *Turning Points: Business Cycles in Canada since 1926*, Toronto: CD Howe Institute, Commentary No. 355, October 2012: 10.

16. Ibid.

17. Karl Marx, "Capital as Fructiferous: Transformation of Surplus Value into Profit," *Grundrisse*, 1857 <https://www.marxists.org/archive/marx/works/1857/grundrisse/ch15.htm> accessed 25 July 2017. For a rich account of capitalism and its crises see James O'Connor, *The Meaning of Crisis*, Oxford: Blackwell, 1987.

18 David Harvey, *Seventeen Contradictions and the End of Capitalism*, New York: Oxford University Press, 2014: 232.

19. James O'Connor, *Natural Causes*.

20. Joel Bakan, *The Corporation*, Toronto: Viking Canada, 2004: 61. Regan Boychuk, "Ralph Klein's multibillion dollar liability is about to blow up in Alberta's face," *National Observer*, 3 April, 2017 <http://www.nationalobserver.com/2017/04/03/analysis/ralph-kleins-multibillion-dollar-liability-about-blow-albertas-face> accessed 26 July 2017. Andrew Nikiforuk, "Energy industry legacy: Hundreds of abandoned wells leaking methane in Alberta communities," *The Tyee*, 28 June 2017 <https://thetyee.ca/News/2017/06/28/Energy-Industry-Legacy/?utm_source=daily&utm_medium=email&utm_campaign=280617> accessed 26 July 2017. Jeremy Nuttall, "Mount Polley disaster brought quick government PR response, documents show," *The Tyee*, 14 July 2017 <https://thetyee.ca/News/2017/07/14/Mount-Polley-Disaster-Government-PR-Response/> accessed 26 July 2017.

21. Jason W. Moore, *Capitalism in the Web of Life: Ecology and the Accumulation of Capital*, London: Verso, 2015: 94–98, 280. Allan Schnaiberg, *The Environment: From Surplus to Scarcity*, New York: Oxford University Press, 1980.

22. Moore, *Capitalism in the Web of Life*: 280–82. Nafeez Mosaddeq Ahmed, *Failing States, Collapsing Systems*, Berlin: Springer, 2017: 32–36. Éric Pineault, "The capitalist pressure to extract, an ecological and political economy of extreme oil in Canada," *Studies in Political Economy* 99, 2018. Fred Magdoff and John Bellamy Foster, *What Every Environmentalist Needs to Know About Capitalism*, New York: Monthly Review Press, 2011: 17.

23. William E. Rees, "Avoiding collapse: An agenda for sustainable degrowth and relocalizing the economy," Vancouver: Canadian Centre for Policy Alternatives, BC Office, 2014.

24. Andreas Malm, *Fossil Capital*, London: Verso, 2016: 17–18, 314, 38–41, 284.

25. Richard Heede, "Tracing anthropogenic carbon dioxide and methane emissions to fossil fuel and cement producers, 1854–2010," *Climate Change* 122, 2014: 229–41. Douglas Starr, "Just 90 companies are to blame for most climate change, this 'carbon accountant' says," *Science*, 25 August 2016 <http://www.sciencemag.org/news/2016/08/just-90-companies-are-blame-most-climate-change-carbon-accountant-says> accessed 27 July 2017. Paul Griffin, CDP *Carbon Majors*

Report 2017, London: CDP, 2017: 8 <https://www.cdp.net/en/reports/archive> accessed 9 August 2017. Damian Carrington, "Fossil fuels subsidised by $10m a minute, says IMF," *The Guardian,* 18 May 2015 <https://www.theguardian.com/environment/2015/may/18/fossil-fuel-companies-getting-10m-a-minute-in-subsidies-says-imf> accessed 2 September 2017.

26. John Urry, *Anatomy of Capitalist Societies,* London: Macmillan, 1981. Ellen Meiksins Wood, "The separation of the economic and the political in capitalism," *New Left Review* 127 (1981): 81. Fred Block, "The ruling class does not rule: Notes on the Marxist Theory of the State," *Socialist Revolution* 7, 3, 1977: 6–28.

27. Bob Jessop, *The State: Past, Present, Future,* Cambridge: Polity Press, 2016: 100. James O'Connor, *The Fiscal Crisis of the State,* New York: St. Martin's Press, 1973.

28. Rianne Mahon, *The Politics of Industrial Restructuring.* Toronto: University of Toronto Press, 1984: 41, 39.

29. Ralph Miliband, "State power and class interests," *New Left Review* 138, 1983: 65.

30. Quintin Hoare and Geoffrey Nowell Smith, "State and civil society," in Quintin Hoare and Geoffrey Nowell Smith (eds.), *Selections from the Prison Notebooks of Antonio Gramsci,* International Publishers, 1971: 208. Urry, *Anatomy,* 31. Marx, *Capital* vol. 1, Chapter 6.

31. Dorothy E. Smith, "Women, class and family," pp. 1–44 in Roxana Ng (ed.), *Women, Class, Family and the State,* Toronto: Garamond Press, 1985: 15, 16–17.

32. Bruce Livesey, "What have the Irvings done to New Brunswick?" *National Observer,* 16 June 2016 <https://www.nationalobserver.com/2016/06/06/news/what-have-irvings-done-new-brunswick> accessed 12 March 2018. Chris Sorenson, "The interview: Jacques Poitras on the Irving family dynasty," *Maclean's,* 29 September 2014 <http://www.macleans.ca/economy/business/the-interview-jacques-poitras-on-the-irving-family-dynasty/> accessed 12 March 2018. J.D. Irving, "History," n.d. <https://www.jdirving.com/jd-irving-about-us-history.aspx> accessed 12 March 2018.

33. Alan Sears, *Retooling the Mind Factory,* Aurora, ON: Garamond Press, 2003: 38–39.

CHAPTER 2 NOTES

1. Joyce Green, "Decolonization and recolonization in Canada," in Wallace Clement and Leah Vosco (eds.), *Changing Canada: Political Economy as Transformation,* Montreal: McGill-Queen's University Press, 2003: 52.

2. Gord Hill, *500 Years of Indigenous Resistance,* Oakland, CA: PM Press, 2009: 43–45. John Porter, *The Vertical Mosaic,* Toronto: University of Toronto Press, 1965. Henry Milner and Sheilagh Hodgins Milner, *The Decolonization of Quebec,* Toronto: McClelland & Stewart, 1973: 75.

3. Jorge Niosi, *Canadian Capitalism,* Toronto: Lorimer, 1981: 67–68. William K. Carroll, *Corporate Power in a Globalizing World,* Don Mills: Oxford University Press, 2010: 17–18.

4. Glen Sean Coulthard, *Red Skin, White Masks,* Minneapolis: University of Minnesota Press, 2014: 7, 8. Gord Hill, *500 Years.*

5. Joyce A. Green, "Towards a détente with history: Confronting Canada's colonial legacy," *International Journal of Canadian Studies* 12 (Fall) 1995: 92.

6. "Hudson's Bay Company History," Archives of Manitoba, <https://www.gov.mb.ca/chc/archives/hbca/about/hbc_history.html> accessed 1 August 2017.

7. Ibid.

8. Gustavus Myers, *A History of Canadian Wealth,* Toronto: James Lorimer, 1975 [1914]: 148. Frank J. Tough, "Aboriginal rights versus the deed of surrender: The legal rights of Native peoples and Canada's Acquisition of the Hudson's Bay Company Territory," *Prairie Forum* 17, 2, 1992: 233 <http://iportal.usask.ca/index.php?cat=276&t=sub_pages> accessed 1 August 2017.

9. H. Claire Pentland, *Labour and Capital in Canada 1650–1860,* Toronto: James Lorimer, 1981.

10. Paul Craven and Tom Traves, "The class politics of the National Policy, 1872–1933," *Journal of Canadian Studies,* 1979.

11. Jason W. Moore, *Capitalism in the Web of Life: Ecology and the Accumulation of Capital,* London: Verso, 2015: 53–54. Stephen Leahy, "Canada is now the world's leading 'deforestation nation,'" *Rabble,* 1 October 2014 <http://rabble.ca/columnists/2014/10/canada-now-worlds-leading-deforestation-nation> accessed 3 August 2017. Laurel Sefton MacDowell, *An Environmental History of Canada,* Vancouver: UBC Press, 2012: 63.

12. Myers, *A History of Canadian Wealth*: 150, 151, 155.

13. <commons.wikimedia.org/wiki/Donald_Alexander_Smith,_1st_Baron_Strathcona_and_Mount_Royal#/media/File:LastSpike_Craigellachie_BC_Canada.jpg>.

14. Alexander Reford, "Smith, Donald Alexander, 1st Baron Strathcona and Mount Royal," in *Dictionary of Canadian Biography,* vol. 14, University of Toronto/Université Laval, 1998 <http://www.biographi.ca/en/bio/smith_donald_alexander_14E.html> accessed 2 August 2017.

15. Karl Marx, *Capital: A Critique of Political Economy, Vol. 1,* translated by Samuel Moore and Edward Aveling, 1887 [1867]: chapter 25 <https://www.marxists.org/archive/marx/works/1867-c1/ch25.htm> accessed 3 August 2017. Richard P. De Grass, "Development of monopolies in Canada from 1907–1913," Master's thesis, University of Waterloo, 1977: 88, 111. J.L. McClelland, "The merger movement in Canada since 1880," Master's thesis, Queen's University, 1929.

16. Rudolf Hilferding, *Finance Capital: A Study of the Latest Phase of Capitalist Development,* London: Routledge & K. Paul: 1981 [1910]. William K. Carroll, *Corporate Power in a Globalizing World: A Study in Elite Social Organization,* Don Mills, ON: Oxford University Press, 2004.

17. Rudolf Hilferding, *Finance Capital,* 119–20.

18. Joel Bakan, *The Corporation,* Toronto: Viking Canada, 2004: 11.

19. Karl Marx, *Capital, Vol. 3,* New York: International Publishers, 1996 [1894]: Chapter 27 <https://www.marxists.org/archive/marx/works/1894-c3/ch27.htm> accessed 3 August 2017.

20. Roderick J. Wood, "Corporation Law," *The Canadian Encyclopedia,* 2013 <http://

www.thecanadianencyclopedia.ca/en/article/corporation-law/> accessed 4 August 2017.

21. William K. Carroll, *Corporate Power and Canadian Capitalism*, Vancouver: UBC Press, 1986: 51–52.

22. Ernest Mandel, *Marxist Economic Theory*, London: Merlin Press, 1968: 411. Carroll, *Corporate Power and Canadian Capitalism*, 53.

23. R.B. Fleming, *The Railway King of Canada: Sir William Mackenzie, 1849–1923*, Vancouver: UBC Press, 2007: 171–72. Libbie Park and Frank Park, *Anatomy of Big Business*, Toronto: Progress Books, 1962: 126–27.

24. N.I. Bukharin, "World Movement of Capital, and Change in the Economic Forms of International Connections," in *Imperialism and World Economy*, New York: International Publishers, 1929: Chapter 7 <https://www.marxists.org/archive/bukharin/works/1917/imperial/07.htm> accessed 6 August 2017.

25. Timothy Mitchell, *Carbon Democracy*, London: Verso, 2011: 68. David McNally, *Another World Is Possible*, second edition, Winnipeg: Arbeiter Ring Publishing, 2006: 204.

26. Kenneth D. Barkin, "Organized capitalism," *Journal of Modern History*, 47, 1, 1975: 125.

27. Alix Granger, "Banking in Canada," *Canadian Encyclopedia*, 2017 <http://www.thecanadianencyclopedia.ca/en/article/banking/> accessed 5 September 2017.

28. Canada, *Report of the Royal Commission on Price Spreads*, Ottawa: King's Printer, 1937: 20–22, 330. Niosi, *Canadian Capitalism*.

29. Gilles Piédalue, "Les groupes financiers au Canada 1900–1930," *Revue d'histoire de l'Amérique française*, 30, 1, 1976: 3–34.

30. Carroll, *Corporate Power and Canadian Capitalism*, 66, 144.

31. Kari Levitt, *Silent Surrender*, Toronto: Macmillan of Canada, 1970.

32. Daniel Drache, "The Canadian bourgeoisie and its national consciousness," in Ian Lumsden (ed.), *Close the 49th Parallel etc: The Americanization of Canada*, Toronto: University of Toronto Press, 1970: 3–25. R.T. Naylor, "The rise and fall of the third commercial empire of the St Lawrence," in Gary Teeple (ed.), *Capitalism and the National Question in Canada*, Toronto: University of Toronto Press, 1972: 1–41. Wallace Clement, *The Canadian Corporate Elite*, Toronto: McClelland & Stewart, 1975. Wallace Clement, *Continental Corporate Power*, Toronto: McClelland & Stewart, 1977.

33. William K. Carroll, "From Canadian corporate elite to transnational capitalist class: Transitions in the organization of corporate power," *Canadian Review of Sociology*, 44,3, 2007: 269. William K. Carroll, "The corporate elite and the transformation of finance capital: A view from Canada," *Sociological Review*, 56, S1, 2008: 44–63. William K. Carroll and Scott Lewis, "Restructuring finance capital: Changes in the Canadian corporate network 1976–1986," *Sociology*, 25, 1991: 491–510. Jorge Niosi, *Canadian Multinationals*, Toronto: Between the Lines, 1985. Jerome Klassen, *Joining Empire*, Toronto: University of Toronto Press, 2014. Paul Kellogg, *Escape from the Staples Trap*, Toronto: University of Toronto Press, 2015.

34. Carroll, *Corporate Power and Canadian Capitalism*, 156.

35. David A. Wolfe, "The rise and demise of the Keynesian era in Canada: Economic

policy, 1930–1982," in Michael S. Cross and Gregory S. Kealey (eds.), *Modern Canada 1930s–1980s*, Toronto: McClelland & Stewart, 1984: 46–49.

36. John Holmes, "Industrial restructuring in a period of crisis: An analysis of the Canadian automobile industry, 1973–83," *Antipode*, 20, 1, 1988: 24.

37. Holmes, "Industrial restructuring," 25–27. David Wolfe, "The rise and demise," 65–76.

38. William K. Carroll, "Undoing the end of history: Canada-centred reflections on the challenge of globalization," in Yildiz Atasoy and William K. Carroll (eds.), *Global Shaping and its Alternatives*, Toronto: Garamond Press, 2003. Scott Lash and John Urry, *The End of Organized Capitalism*, Madison, WI: University of Wisconsin Press, 1987: 5–7, 229–31.

39. Jordan Brennan, *A Shrinking Universe: How Concentrated Corporate Capital Is Shaping Income Inequality in Canada*, Ottawa: Canadian Centre for Policy Alternatives, November, 2012: 19–20 <https://www.policyalternatives.ca/publications/reports/shrinking-universe> accessed 5 September 2017.

40. Ibid, figure 6, p. 20. Reprinted with permission of CCPA.

41. David Macdonald, *Outrageous Fortune: Documenting Canada's Wealth Gap*, Ottawa: Canadian Centre for Policy Alternatives, 2014.

42. Brennan, *A Shrinking Universe*, 40, 29.

43. Brennan, *A Shrinking Universe*, 26, figure 8.

44. Francine Kopun, "Loblaw, Walmart, Sobeys, Metro, Giant Tiger allegedly involved in alleged bread price-fixing scheme: Court documents," *Toronto Star*, 31 January 2018 <https://www.thestar.com/business/2018/01/31/at-least-7-companies-committed-indictable-offences-in-bread-price-fixing-scandal-competition-bureau.html> accessed 2 March 2018. Jason Markusoff, "Loblaw's price-fixing may have cost you at least $400," *Maclean's*, 11 January 2018 <http://www.macleans.ca/economy/economicanalysis/14-years-of-loblaws-bread-price-fixing-may-have-cost-you-at-least-400/> accessed 2 March 2018. *Canadian Business*, "Canada's Richest People 2018," 9 November 2017. <http://www.canadianbusiness.com/lists-and-rankings/richest-people/top-25-richest-canadians-2018/image/24/> accessed 2 March 2018.

45. Brennan, *A Shrinking Universe*, 39.

46. Carroll, *Corporate Power in a Globalizing World*, 93–96.

47. Brennan, *A Shrinking Universe*, 38, figure 17·

48. Carroll, *Corporate Power in a Globalizing World*, 96.

CHAPTER 3 NOTES

1. William K. Carroll, "The changing face(s) of corporate power in Canada," in Edward G. Grabb and Monica Hwang (eds.), *Social Inequality in Canada*, 6th edition, Toronto: Oxford University Press, 2016: 12.

2. Victor Perlo, "'People's Capitalism' and stock ownership," *American Economic Review*, 48, 1958: 333–47. John Scott, *Corporate Business and Capitalist Classes*, New York: Oxford University Press, 1997.

3. William K. Carroll, *Corporate Power in a Globalizing World*, Toronto: Oxford

University Press, 2004: 5.

4. Beth Mintz and Michael Schwartz, *The Power Structure of American Business*, Chicago: University of Chicago Press, 1985. Carroll, *Corporate Power in a Globalizing World*, 5.

5. Carroll, *Corporate Power in a Globalizing World*, 5–6. Henk Overbeek, "Finance capital and the crisis in Britain," *Capital & Class*, 2, 1980: 102.

6. snc-Lavalin, *Annual Report 2015*, Montréal: snc-Lavalin, 2016.

7. S.A. Marglin, "What do bosses do? The origins and functions of hierarchy in Capitalist production," *Review of Radical Political Economics*, 6, 2, 1974: 84. Karl Marx and Frederick Engels, "Bourgeois and proletarians," in *Manifesto of the Communist Party*, Marx/Engels Internet Archive, 2000 [1848]: Chapter I <https://www.marxists.org/archive/marx/works/1848/communist-manifesto/ch01.htm#007> accessed 14 August 2017.

8. Norene Pupo and Mark Thomas, "Work in the new economy: Critical reflections," in Noreen Pupo and Mark Thomas (eds.), *Interrogating the New Economy: Restructuring Work in the 21st Century*, Toronto: University of Toronto Press, 2009: xiii.

9. Tom Malleson, *Fired Up About Capitalism*, Toronto: Between the Lines, 2016: 54. Lisa VeneKlasen and Valerie Miller, *A New Weave of Power, People, and Politics*, Warwickshire, UK: Practical Action Pub, 2007.

10. James W. Rinehart, *The Tyranny of Work*, Toronto: Longman, 1975: 19, 44.

11. Graham S. Lowe, "Class, job and gender in the Canadian office," *Labour/Le Travail*, 10, 1982: 15, 17. Richard Edwards, *Contested Terrain*, New York: Basic Books, 1979: 13.

12. Created from data from Orbis (Bureau van Dijk) and Corporate Mapping Project.

13. Antonio Gramsci, "The intellectuals," in *Selections from the Prison Notebooks*, New York: International Publishers, 1971: 14.

14. Antonio Gramsci, *Selections from the Prison Notebooks*, London: Lawrence and Wishart, 1971.

15. Hugh Mackenzie, *Throwing Money at the Problem: 10 years of Executive Compensation in Canada*, Ottawa: Canadian Centre for Policy Alternatives, 3 January 2017 <https://www.policyalternatives.ca/ceo2017> accessed 17 August 2017. Erik Olin Wright, *Classes*, London: Verso, 1985.

16. Hugh Mackenzie, *Throwing Money*, 12. Reprinted with permission.

17. Edwards, *Contested Terrain*, 146.

18. Gary Gereffi and Miguel Korzeniewicz, *Commodity Chains and Global Capitalism*, Westport, CT: Greenwood Press/Praeger, 1994. Jennifer Bair, "Editor's introduction: Commodity chains in and of the world system," *Journal of World-Systems Research*, 20, 2014: 1–10.

19. William I. Robinson, *A Theory of Global Capitalism*, Baltimore: Johns Hopkins University Press, 2004: 17–18, 15.

20. Jenny Chan, Xu Lizhi, and Yang *La machine est ton seigneur et ton maître*, Marseille: Agone, 2015.

21. Kenan Erçel, "Orientalization of exploitation: A class-analytical critique of the sweatshop discourse," *Rethinking Marxism*, 18, 2, 2006: 289–306.

22. Tarannum Kamlani, "Made in Bangladesh," *The Fifth Estate,* CBC *Radio-Canada,* 2013 <http://www.cbc.ca/fifth/episodes/2013-2014/made-in-bangladesh> accessed 15 August 2017.

23. Deborah Barndt, *Tangled Routes,* second edition, Toronto: Rowman & Littlefield, 2008: 261. Jason W. Moore, *Capitalism in the Web of Life: Ecology and the Accumulation of Capital,* London: Verso, 2015: 17. Barndt, *Tangled Routes,* 266–67.

24. Barndt, *Tangled Routes,* 265, 269.

25. Larry Elliott, "Can the world economy survive without fossil fuels?" *The Guardian,* 8 April 2015 <https://www.theguardian.com/news/2015/apr/08/can-world-economy-survive-without-fossil-fuels> accessed 26 October 2017. <http://www.corporatemapping.ca/>.

26. Éric Pineault, "The capitalist pressure to extract, an ecological and political economy of extreme oil in Canada," *Studies in Political Economy* 99, 2018. Angela V. Carter and Anna Zalik, "Fossil capitalism and the rentier state: Toward a political ecology of Alberta's oil economy," in Laurie E. Adkin (ed.), *First World Petro-Politics: The Political Ecology and Governance of Alberta,* Toronto: University of Toronto Press, 2016: 52–77. National Energy Board, "Estimated production of Canadian crude oil and equivalent," 2017 <http://www.neb-one.gc.ca/nrg/sttstc/crdlndptrlmprdct/stt/stmtdprdctn-eng.html> accessed 29 October 2017.

27. Geoffrey McCormack and Thom Workman, *The Servant State,* Winnipeg and Halifax: Fernwood, 2015: 32. Larissa Stendie and Laurie E. Adkin, "In the path of the pipeline: Environmental citizenship, Aboriginal rights, and the Northern Gateway Pipeline Review," in Laurie E. Adkin (ed.), *First World Petro-Politics: The Political Ecology and Governance of Alberta,* Toronto: University of Toronto Press, 2016: 417.

28. Originally published on DeSmog Canada <www.desmog.org> 2 July 2014, reprinted with permission of Alex McLean.

29. Greg Albo and Lilian Yap, "From the Tar Sands to 'green jobs'? Work and ecological justice," *The Bullet,* 1280, 12 July 2016 <https://socialistproject.ca/bullet/1280.php> accessed 16 August 2017. Angele Alook, Nicole Hill and Ian Hussey, "Ten things to know about Indigenous people and resource extraction in Alberta," *Corporate Mapping Project,* 21 June 2017 <http://www.corporatemapping.ca/ten-things-to-know-about-indigenous-people-and-resource-extraction-in-alberta/> accessed 16 August 2017.

30. Alook, Hill, and Hussey, "Ten things to know."

31. Gordon Laxer, *After the Sands,* Madeira Park, BC: Douglas & McIntyre, 2015: 165, reprinted with permission of the authors, Gordon Laxer and Petr Cizek.

CHAPTER 4 NOTES

1. John Scott, *Corporate Business and Capitalist Classes,* New York: Oxford University Press, 1997: 40. William K. Carroll, *Corporate Power in a Globalizing World,* Toronto: Oxford University Press, 2004: 42.

2. John Porter, *The Vertical Mosaic,* Toronto: University of Toronto Press, 1965: 591–95. Jorge Niosi, *The Economy of Canada: Who Controls It?* Montreal: Black

Rose Books, 1978. Yoser Gadhoum, "Power of ultimate controlling owners: A survey of Canadian landscape," *Journal of Management Governance*, 10, 2006: 186.

3. John Scott, *Corporate Business*, 47–50.
4. Caroline Cakebread, "Global warming," *Benefits Canada*, 30, 4, 2006: 61–63. CPP Investment Board, Canadian Publicly-Traded Equity Holdings <http://www.cppib.com/documents/1604/cdn_publicequityholdings_Mar2017_en.htm> accessed 17 August 2017. CPP Investment Board, Foreign Publicly-Traded Equity Holdings <http://www.cppib.com/documents/1606/foreign_publicequityholdings_Mar2017_en.htm> accessed 17 August 2017.
5. Rick Baert, "10 largest Canadian public pension funds' assets top $1 trillion — report," *Pensions and Investments*, 10, December, 2015 <http://www.pionline.com/article/20151210/ONLINE/151219992/10-largest-canadian-public-pension-funds-assets-top-1-trillion-8212-report> accessed 17 August 2017. Statistics Canada, "Gross domestic product, expenditure-based," 2017 <http://www.statcan.gc.ca/tables-tableaux/sum-som/l01/cst01/econ04-eng.htm> accessed 21 August 2017.
6. Carroll, *Corporate Power in a Globalizing World*, 64–65.
7. "Power Corporation of Canada organization chart" <https://www.powercorporation.com/en/companies/organization-chart/> accessed 18 August 2017. "Canada's richest people: The complete Top 100 ranking," *Canadian Business*, 7 December 2017 <http://www.canadianbusiness.com/lists-and-rankings/richest-people/100-richest-canadians-complete-list/> accessed 5 March 2018. "Power Corporation of Canada financial highlights" <https://www.powercorporation.com/en/investors/financial-highlights/> accessed 18 August 2017.
8. <powercorporation.com/en/companies/organization-chart/>.
9. "Power Corporation of Canada organization chart." "LafargeHolcim board of directors" <http://www.lafargeholcim.com/board-directors> accessed 18 August 2017. "GBL Management" <http://www.gbl.be/en/team> accessed 18 August 2017.
10. Created from data from Orbis (Bureau van Dijk) and Corporate Mapping Project.
11. "We've accomplished a lot in seven decades," 2017 <https://www.transcanada.com/en/about/our-history/> accessed 19 August 2017. The Canadian Press, "A chronological history of controversial Keystone XL pipeline project," CBC *News*, January 24, 2017 <http://www.cbc.ca/news/politics/keystone-xl-pipeline-timeline-1.3950156> accessed 12 September 2017.
12. TransCanada Corporation, "TransCanada completes acquisition of Columbia Pipeline Groups and announces exchange date for subscription receipts," press release, 2016 <https://www.transcanada.com/en/announcements/2016-07-01transcanada-completes-acquisition-of-columbia-pipeline-group-and-announces-exchange-date-for-subscription-receipts/> accessed 19 August 2017. Data in the table are from ORBIS, accessed 19 August 2017.
13. Created from data from ORBIS (Bureau van Dijk) and Corporate Mapping Project.
14. ORBIS, supplemented, where data are newer, with <http://quote.morningstar.ca/Quicktakes/owners/MajorShareholders.

aspx?t=CVE&region=CAN&culture=en-CA> accessed 18 August 2017.

15. TransCanada Corporation, *Management Information Circular*, 27 February 2017 <https://www.transcanada.com/en/about/governance/> accessed 19 August 2017, p. 90.

16. Created from data from ORBIS (Bureau van Dijk) and Corporate Mapping Project.

17. Michael Useem, *The Inner Circle*, Oxford University Press: New York, 1984.

18. Beth Mintz and Michael Schwartz, *The Power Structure of American Business*, Chicago: University of Chicago Press, 1985: 96. World Bank, "5-Bank Asset Concentration for Canada [DDOI06CAA156NWDB]," 11 September 2017, retrieved from FRED, Federal Reserve Bank of St. Louis <https://fred.stlouisfed.org/series/DDOI06CAA156NWDB>.

19. Athar Hussein, "Hilferding's finance capital," *Bulletin of the Conference of Socialist Economists*, 5, 1, 1976: 11. "Fictitious Capital," *Marxist Internet Archive*, n.d. <https://www.marxists.org/glossary/terms/f/i.htm> accessed 22 August 2017. Doug Henwood, "Financial crisis averted?" *Left Business Observer*, 56, December 1992 <http://www.leftbusinessobserver.com/Financial-crisis-averted.html> accessed 22 August 2017. For a contemporary analysis see Cédric Durand, *Fictitious Capital: How Finance Is Appropriating Our Future*, New York: Verso, 2017.

20. Francine Kopun, "Sears Canada pensioners demand shortfall be paid off first," Toronto *Star*, 26 October 2017 <https://www.thestar.com/business/2017/10/26/sears-canada-pensioners-demand-shortfall-be-paid-off-first.html> accessed 26 October 2017. Holly Shaw, "Sears retirees seek trustee to help recoup part of $3 billion in dividends paid to shareholders," *Financial Post*, 14 February 2018 <http://business.financialpost.com/news/retail-marketing/sears-retirees-seek-appointment-of-trustee-to-help-recoup-part-of-the-3b-in-dividends-paid-to-shareholders> accessed 7 March 2018. "Even though Sears Canada is closing, execs will receive bonuses," *Insurance Hunter.ca*, 20 October 2017 <http://www.insurancehunter.ca/news/even-though-sears-canada-closing-execs-will-receive-bonuses> accessed 26 October 2017.

21. Stephen Gill and David Law, "The power of capital: Direct and structural," in Stephen Gill, *Power and Resistance in the New World Order*, New York: Palgrave Macmillan, 2003: 104.

22. Shannon Daub and Bill Carroll, "Why is the CEO of a big Canadian bank giving speeches about climate change and pipelines?" *Corporate Mapping Project*, 6 October, 2016 <http://www.corporatemapping.ca/rbc-ceo-speech-climate-pipelines/> accessed 21 August 2017.

23. Ibid.

24. Ibid.

25. Ibid.

26. <www.corporatemapping.ca/wp-content/uploads/2016/10/RBC-interlocks-FINAL-768x393.png>, reprinted with permission.

CHAPTER 5 NOTES

1. John Porter, *The Vertical Mosaic*, Toronto: University of Toronto Press, 1965: 255. G. William Domhoff, *Who Rules America?* New York: McGraw-Hill, 2006: 21.
2. Gaetano Mosca, *The Ruling Class*, McGraw-Hill, 1939: 53. Bruce Kogut (ed.), *The Small Worlds of Corporate Governance*, Boston: MIT Press, 2012.
3. Michael D. Ornstein, "The social organization of the Canadian capitalist class in comparative perspective," *Canadian Review of Sociology and Anthropology*, 26, 1989: 169–70.
4. William K. Carroll, "The corporate elite and the transformation of finance capital: A view from Canada," *Sociological Review*, 56, S1, 2008: 54–56.
5. William K. Carroll, *Corporate Power in a Globalizing World*, Toronto: Oxford University Press, 2004: 85. Jamie Brownlee, *Ruling Canada*, Halifax and Winnipeg: Fernwood Publishing, 2005, 68.
6. Frank Parkin, *Marxism and Class Theory: A Bourgeois Critique*, London: Tavistock Publications, 1979: 44. Carroll, *Corporate Power*, 24, 18, 40.
7. Jorge Niosi, *The Economy of Canada: Who Controls It?* Montreal: Black Rose Books, 1978.
8. Carroll, *Corporate Power in a Globalizing World*, 21. Reprinted with permission.
9. Karl Marx, *The Poverty of Philosophy*, Marx/Engels Internet Archive, 1999 [1847], Chapter 2 <https://www.marxists.org/archive/marx/works/1847/poverty-philosophy/ch02e.htm> accessed 11 August 2017.
10. Antonio Gramsci, *Selections from the Prison Notebooks*, New York: International Publishers, 1971. Carroll, *Corporate Power in a Globalizing World*, 8.
11. Carroll, *Corporate Power in a Globalizing World*, 4. Reprinted with permission.
12. Michael Useem, *The Inner Circle*, New York: Oxford University Press, 1984: 38. Brownlee, *Ruling Canada*, 56.
13. Gilles Piédalue, "Les groupes financiers au Canada 1900–1930," *Revue d'histoire de l'Amérique française*, 30, 1, 1976: 28. Carroll, *Corporate Power and Canadian Capitalism*, 131.
14. Ornstein, "The social organization," 169–70. William K. Carroll and Malcolm Alexander, "Finance capital and capitalist class integration in the 1990s: Networks of interlocking directorships in Canada and Australia," *Canadian Review of Sociology and Anthropology*, 36, 1999: 341.
15. Harry W. Arthurs, "The hollowing out of corporate Canada?" In Jane Jenson and Boaventura de Sousa Santos (eds.), *Globalizing Institutions: Case Studies in Regulation and Innovation*, Burlington, VT: Ashgate Publishing Company, 2000: 44.
16. William K. Carroll and Jerome Klassen, "Hollowing out corporate Canada? Changes in the Corporate Network since the 1990s," *Canadian Journal of Sociology*, 35, 2010: 13–14.
17. Ibid., 16, 24.
18. Jerome Klassen and William K. Carroll, "Transnational Class Formation? Globalization and the Canadian Corporate Network," *Journal of World-Systems Research*, 17, 2011: 399–400.

19. Potash Corp was renamed Nutrien after it acquired Calgary-based agro-chemical giant Agrium in January 2018.
20. Created from data from ORBIS (Bureau van Dijk) and Corporate Mapping Project.
21. William K. Carroll, "Canada's carbon-capital elite: A tangled web of corporate power," *Canadian Journal of Sociology*, 42, 3, 2017: 253.
22. Porter, *The Vertical Mosaic*, 304–305. Wallace Clement, *The Canadian Corporate Elite*, Toronto: McClelland & Stewart, 1975. Carroll, *Corporate Power in a Globalizing World*, 31, 210–11.
23. Useem, *The Inner Circle*. Carroll, *Corporate Power in a Globalizing World*, 210.

CHAPTER 6 NOTES

1. Tom Engelhardt, "As GM goes, so goes…" *The Nation*, 23 February 2009 <https://www.thenation.com/article/gm-goes-so-goes/> accessed 22 February 2018.
2. John Porter, *The Vertical Mosaic*, Toronto: University of Toronto Press, 1965. Wallace Clement, *The Canadian Corporate Elite*, Toronto: McClelland & Stewart, 1975. John Fox and Michael D. Ornstein, "The Canadian State and Corporate Elites in the Post-War Period," *Canadian Review of Sociology and Anthropology*, 23, 1986: 481–506. William K. Carroll, *Corporate Power in a Globalizing World*, Don Mills: Oxford University Press, 2004. Jamie Brownlee, 2005, *Ruling Canada*, Halifax and Winnipeg: Fernwood Publishing, 2005.
3. William K. Carroll, Nicolas Graham, Michael Lang, Kevin McCarthy, and Zoe Yunker, "Carbon capital's reach into civil society: Architecture of climate-change denialism," *Canadian Review of Sociology*, 54, 3 (forthcoming, August 2018).
4. Ibid.
5. Brownlee, *Ruling Canada*, 81. Peter C. Newman, *Titans: How the New Canadian Establishment Seized Power*, Toronto: Viking, 1998: 151.
6. Brownlee, *Ruling Canada*, 95. G. William Domhoff, *Who Rules America?* Fifth edition, New York: McGraw-Hill, 2005: 77–78.
7. CD Howe Institute, *Lifting Living Standards One Donation at a Time: Report on Giving 2017*, Toronto, 2017: 4–5.
8. Fraser Institute, *2016 Annual Report*, Vancouver, 16–17.
9. Alexis Stoymenoff, "'Charitable' Fraser Institute accepted $500K in foreign funding from Koch oil billionnaires," Vancouver *Observer*, April 25, 2012 <https://www.vancouverobserver.com/politics/2012/04/25/charitable-fraser-institute-accepted-500k-foreign-funding-oil-billionaires> accessed 2 February 2018.
10. <https://www.cdhowe.org/>. <https://www.cdhowe.org/policy-impact> accessed 29 August 2017. Niels Veldhuis, "Fraser Institute ranked top think-tank in Canada, 11th best independent think-tank worldwide," Fraser Institute, 2017 <https://www.fraserinstitute.org/studies/fraser-institute-ranked-top-think-tank-in-canada-11th-best-independent-think-tank-worldwide> accessed 29 August 2017. <https://www.atlasnetwork.org/> accessed 29 August 2017. <https://www.fraserinstitute.org/about/experts> accessed 29 August 2017. <https://www.fraserinstitute.org/education-programs> accessed 29 August 2017.
11. Fox and Ornstein, "The Canadian state," 481–506. Brownlee, *Ruling Canada*,

113–21.

12. William K. Carroll, Nicolas Graham, and Zoë Yunker, 2018, "Carbon Capital and Corporate Influence: Mapping Elite Networks of Corporations, Universities and Research Institutes," in Jamie Brownlee, Christopher Hurl and Kevin Walby (eds.), *Corporatizing Canada: Making Business out of Public Service*, Toronto: Between the Lines. Jamie Brownlee, *Academia, Inc: How Corporatization Is Transforming Canadian Universities*, Halifax: Fernwood Publishing, 2015: 16. William K. Carroll and James Beaton, "Globalization, Neo-Liberalism, and the Changing Face of Corporate Hegemony in Higher Education," *Studies in Political Economy*, 62, 1, 2000: 71–98. Trevor Cole, "Ivy-League Hustle," *Report on Business Magazine*, 14, 12, 1998: 34–44. Canadian Association of University Teachers, *Open for Business — On What Terms? An Analysis of 12 Collaborations between Canadian Universities and Corporations, Donors and Governments*, November 2013 <http://www.caut. ca/docs/default-source/academic-freedom/open-for-business-%28nov-2013%29. pdf?sfvrsn=4> accessed 2 September 2017.

13. David Langille, "The Business Council on National Issues and the Canadian state," *Studies in Political Economy*, 24, 1987: 41–85. Murray Dobbin, *The Myth of the Good Corporate Citizen: Democracy Under the Rule of Big Business*, Toronto: Stoddart, 1998. William K. Carroll and Murray Shaw, "Consolidating a neoliberal policy bloc in Canada, 1976–1996." *Canadian Public Policy*, 27, 2, 2001: 1–23. Donald Gutstein, *Harperism: How Stephen Harper and his think tanks colleagues have transformed Canada*," Toronto: Lorimer, 2014.

14. Calculations by the authors, from the Federal Lobbyist Registry.

15. Nicolas Graham, Shannon Daub, and Bill Carroll, *Mapping Political Influence: Political Donations and Lobbying by the Fossil Fuel Industry in BC*, Vancouver: Canadian Centre for Policy Alternatives, 2017: 27.

16. Leo Panitch "The development of corporatism in liberal democracies," *Comparative Political Studies*, 10, 1, 1977: 61–90. David A. Nock, "The intimate connection: Links between the political and economic systems in Canadian federal politics," doctoral dissertation, University of Alberta, 1976: 5. Office of the Senate Ethics Officer, "Conflict of Interest Code for Senators," Senate of Canada, 2014 <sen. parl.gc.ca/seo-cse/PDF/Code-e.pdf> accessed 30 August 2017.

17. William K. Carroll, "Corporate interests displace the public interest: Only business leaders chosen for Economic Advisory Council," *CCPA Monitor*, 16, 1, 2009: 26–29. "Minister Morneau announces membership of the Advisory Council on Economic Growth," Ottawa: Department of Finance, 18 March 2016 <http://www.fin.gc.ca/ n16/16-031-eng.asp> accessed 30 August 2017. Advisory Council on Economic Growth, *Unleashing Productivity through Infrastructure*, 2017 <www.budget.gc.ca/ aceg-ccce/pdf/infrastructure-eng.pdf> accessed 30 August 2017.

18. James Kwak, "Cultural capture and the financial crisis," in Daniel Carpenter and David Moss (eds.), *Preventing Regulatory Capture: Special Interest Influence and How to Limit It*, Cambridge University Press, 2014: 73 <http:// www.tobinproject.org/sites/tobinproject.org/files/assets/Kwak%20-%20 Cultural%20Capture%20and%20the%20Financial%20Crisis.pdf> accessed 30 August 2017. James Wilt, "Alberta's pipeline regulation a 'facade': experts,"

Desmog Canada, 23 March 2017 <https://www.desmog.ca/2017/03/23/alberta-s-pipeline-regulation-facade-experts?utm_source=Newsletter&utm_medium=DSCWeekly&utm_campaign=March_30_2017> accessed 30 August 2017. Andrew Nikiforuk, "On oil spills, Alberta regulator can't be believed: New report," *The Tyee*, 9 February 2017 <https://thetyee.ca/News/2017/02/09/Oil-Spills-Alberta-Regulator/> accessed 30 August 2017.

19. Shawn McCarthy, "National Energy Board needs major overhaul, panel says," Toronto *Globe and Mail*, 15 May 2017 <https://beta.theglobeandmail.com/report-on-business/industry-news/energy-and-resources/dismantle-neb-create-bodies-for-regulation-growth-panel/article34989230/?ref=http://www.theglobeandmail.com&> accessed 12 September 2017. Government of Canada, *A Modern, New and World-Class Federal Energy Regulator for the 21st Century*, Ottawa, 2018.

20. Jeff Nesbit, *Poison Tea: How Big Oil and Big Tobacco Invested the Tea Party and Captured the GOP*, New York: St. Martin's Press, 2016: 8–16 <http://www.energycitizens.ca/> accessed 31 August 2017.

21. Canadian Association of Petroleum Producers <http://www.energycitizens.ca/>.

22. Mediatoil.ca <http://mediatoil.ca/Documents/Details/2161>. Used with permission from CAPP.

23. John Hilary, *The Poverty of Capitalism*, London: Pluto Press, 2013: 59, 79. Government of Canada <http://www.international.gc.ca/csr_counsellor-conseiller_rse/index.aspx?lang=eng> accessed 31 August 2017.

24. Shane Gunster and Paul Saurette, "Storylines in the sands: News, narrative and ideology in the Calgary Herald," *Canadian Journal of Communication*, 39, 3, 2014: 333–59. Kathleen Raso and Robert Joseph Neubauer, "Managing dissent: Energy pipelines and 'new right' politics in Canada," *Canadian Journal of Communication*, 41, 1, 2016: 118.

25. David Model, *Corporate Rule*, Montreal: Black Rose Books, 2003: 128. Robert A. Hackett and William K. Carroll, *Remaking Media: The Struggle to Democratize Public Communication*, New York: Routledge, 2006: 28, 16. Dwayne Winseck, "Poster: Mapping Canada's top telecoms, internet & media companies by revenue and market share (2015)," Canadian Media Concentration Research Project, 22 November 2016 <http://www.cmcrp.org/poster-mapping-canadas-top-telecoms-internet-media-companies-by-revenue-and-market-share-2015/> accessed 12 September 2017.

26. Dallas Smythe, *Counterclockwise*, Boulder, CO: Westview Press, 1994: 250. Christian Fuchs, "Dallas Smythe today — the audience commodity, the digital labour debate, Marxist political economy and critical theory. Prolegomena to a digital labour theory of value," *tripleC*, 10, 2, 2012: 720–21.

27. Jodi Dean, *The Communist Horizon*, London: Verso, 2013: 125–26.

28. Matthew T. Huber, *Lifeblood: Oil, Freedom, and the Forces of Capital*, Minneapolis: University of Minnesota Press, 2013, pp. 76–81.

29. Andrew Gamble, *The Free Economy and the Strong State*, New York: Macmillan, 1988. David Hughes, "Can Canada expand oil and gas production, build pipelines and keep its climate change commitments?" Vancouver: Canadian Centre for

Policy Alternatives, 2016. <https://www.policyalternatives.ca/more-than-enough> accessed 13 September 2017.

30. Gregory Albo and Carlo Fanelli, "Austerity against democracy: An authoritarian phase of neoliberalism?" *Teoria Critica* 4, 2014: 21–22.

31. Public Safety Canada, *Action Plan for Critical Infrastructure (2014–2017)*, 2014 <https://www.publicsafety.gc.ca/cnt/rsrcs/pblctns/pln-crtcl-nfrstrctr-2014-17/index-en.aspx>, accessed 2 September 2017. Carole Linnittemists" threat to government and industry," *DeSmogCanada* 17 February 2015, "LEAKED: Internal RCMP document names "violent anti-petroleum extr<https://www.desmog.ca/2015/02/17/leaked-internal-rcmp-document-names-anti-petroleum-extremists-threat-government-industry>, accessed 2 September 2017. Elizabeth Rowley, "Bill C-59: Another threat to democracy," *People's Voice* 29 June 2017 <http://peoplesvoice.ca/2017/06/29/bill-c-59-another-threat-to-democracy/>, accessed 2 September 2017.

32. Public Safety Canada, *National Strategy for Critical Infrastructure*, 2017 <https://www.publicsafety.gc.ca/cnt/rsrcs/pblctns/srtg-crtcl-nfrstrctr/index-en.aspx>, accessed 22 August 2017. Bruce Livesey, "Spies in our midst: RCMP and CSIS snoop on green activists," *National Observer* 5 May 2017, <http://www.nationalobserver.com/2017/05/05/news/spies-our-midst-rcmp-and-csis-snoop-green-activists>, accessed 2 September 2017.

CHAPTER 7 NOTES

1. Elaine Coburn and Cliff (Kam'ayaam/Chachim'multhnii) Atleo, "Not just another social movement: Indigenous resistance and resurgence," in William K. Carroll and Kanchan Sarker (eds.), *A World to Win: Contemporary Social Movements and Counter-Hegemony*, Winnipeg: ARP Books, 2016: 178–79, 190.

2. Ian McKay, *Rebels, Reds, Radicals: Rethinking Canada's Left History*, Toronto: Between the Lines, 2005: 32. "Labour Force Survey, August 2017," *Statistics Canada Daily*, 8 September 2017 <http://www.statcan.gc.ca/daily-quotidien/170908/dq170908a-eng.htm> accessed 12 September 2017. Amy Minsky, "Average hourly wages in Canada have barely budged in 40 years," *Global News*, 15 June 2017 <http://globalnews.ca/news/3531614/average-hourly-wage-canada-stagnant/> accessed 12 September 2017.

3. McKay, *Rebels, Reds, Radicals*, 25, 32–33.

4. Lisa VeneKlasen and Valerie Miller, *A New Weave of Power, People, and Politics: The Action for Advocacy and Citizen Participation*, Warwickshire, U.K.: Practical Action Pub., 2007.

5. Robert Albritton, *Economics Transformed: Discovering the Brilliance of Marx*, London: Pluto Press, 2007: 163, 164.

6. John Restakis, *Humanizing the Economy: Co-operatives in the Age of Capital*, Gabriola Island, BC: New Society Publishers, 2010: 3, 238–39.

7. Chris Rogers, *Capitalism and its Alternatives*, London: Zed Books, 2014: 99.

8. James Rowe, Ana Maria Peredo, and John Restakis, "How the NDP and Greens can grow BC's cooperative economy," *The Tyee*, 27 July 2017 <https://thetyee.

ca/Opinion/2017/07/27/BC-NDP-Greens-Can-Grow-Co-op-Economy/?utm_
source=daily&utm_medium=email&utm_campaign=270717> accessed 14
September 2017. "Record-breaking CEO pay now 209 times more than average
worker," Canadian Centre for Policy Alternatives, 2 January 2018 <https://www.
policyalternatives.ca/newsroom/news-releases/record-breaking-ceo-pay-now-
209-times-more-average-worker> accessed 6 March 2018.

9. "Balanced jobs," *Participatory Economics: A Model for a New Economy*, n.d.
<http://www.participatoryeconomics.info/institutions/balanced-jobs/> accessed
14 September 2017.

10. Gregory Albo, "Democratic citizenship and the future of public management," in
Gregory Albo, David Langille and Leo Panitch (eds.), *A Different Kind of State?*
Popular Power and Democratic Administration, Toronto: Oxford University Press,
1993: 31.

11. *Unburnable Carbon 2013: Wasted Capital and Stranded Assets*, Carbon Tracker
Initiative and the Grantham Research Institute on Climate Change and the
Environment. Jessica Lukawiecki and Laura Gosset, "Taking climate on board:
Are Canadian energy and utilities company boards equipped to address climate
change?" Vancouver: Shareholder Association for Research & Education, January,
2017: 9 <https://share.ca/publications/issue-briefs/> accessed 14 September 2017.

12. Tom Malleson, *Fired up about Capitalism*, Toronto: Between the Lines, 2016:
85–86.

13. Robin Blackburn, "A visionary pragmatist," *Counterpunch*, 22 December 2005.
<https://www.counterpunch.org/2005/12/22/a-visonary-pragmatist/> accessed
14 September 2017. Rudolf Meidner, "Why did the Swedish model fail?" in Ralph
Miliband and Leo Panitch (eds), *Socialist Register 1993*, London: Merlin Press,
1993: 225.

14. *The Regina Manifesto (1933) Co-operative Commonwealth Federation Programme*
<http://www.socialisthistory.ca/Docs/CCF/ReginaManifesto.htm> accessed
15 September 2017. Leo Panitch, "From the global crisis to Canada's crisis,"
Toronto *Globe and Mail*, 4 December 2008 <https://beta.theglobeandmail.com/
opinion/from-the-global-crisis-to-canadas-crisis/article22502333/?ref=http://
www.theglobeandmail.com&> accessed 16 September 2017. Richard Swift,
S.O.S. Alternatives to Capitalism, Toronto: Between the Lines, 2014: 153. David
Macdonald, *The Big Banks' Big Secret: Estimating Government Support for
Canadian Banks During the Financial Crisis*, Ottawa: Canadian Centre for Policy
Alternatives, 30 April 2012: 6–7 <https://www.policyalternatives.ca/publications/
reports/big-banks-big-secret> accessed 15 September 2017.

15. Karl Marx, "Theses on Feurbach," in William K. Carroll (ed.), *Critical Strategies
for Social Research*, Toronto: Canadian Scholar's Press, 2004 [1845]: 22. Marta
Harnecker, *A World to Build*, New York: Monthly Review Press, 2015: 93.

16. Transnational Institute, "Participatory budgeting in Canada," 1 February 2006
<https://www.tni.org/es/node/13963#10> accessed 15 September 2017.

17. "Alternative Federal Budget," <https://www.policyalternatives.ca/projects/
alternative-federal-budget> accessed 15 September 2017.

18. James Tobin, "The case for a tax on international monetary transactions," CCPA

Monitor, 1 April 2011 <https://www.policyalternatives.ca/publications/monitor/tobin-tax> accessed 15 September 2017. Thomas I. Palley, "Destabilizing speculation and the case for an international currency transactions tax," *Global Policy Forum*, June 2000 <https://www.globalpolicy.org/social-and-economic-policy/global-taxes-1-79/currency-transaction-taxes/45990-destabilizing-speculation-and-the-case-for-an-international-currency-transactions-tax.html> accessed 15 September 2017. Robert Pollin, Dean Baker, and Marc Schaberg, *Securities Transaction Taxes for US Financial Markets*, PERI Working Paper No. 20, 2002 <https://papers.ssrn.com/sol3/papers.cfm?abstract_id=333742> accessed 15 September 2017.

19. "What is fossil fuel divestment?" <https://gofossilfree.org/what-is-fossil-fuel-divestment/> accessed 15 September 2017. Desmond Tutu, "We need an apartheid-style boycott to save the planet," *The Guardian,* 10 April 2014 <https://www.theguardian.com/commentisfree/2014/apr/10/divest-fossil-fuels-climate-change-keystone-xl> accessed 15 September 2017. James Rowe, Jessica Dempsey, and Emilia Belliveau-Thompson, "Fossil fuel divestment, non-reformist reforms and anti-capitalist strategy," in William K. Carroll (ed.), *Regime of Obstruction: How Corporate Power Blocks Energy Democracy*, Edmonton: Athabasca University Press, forthcoming. Gregory Albo and Lilian Yap, "From the tar sands to 'green jobs'? Work and ecological justice," *The Bullet* 1280, 12 July 2016 <https://socialistproject.ca/bullet/1280.php> accessed 15 September 2017.

20. Jordan Kinder, "The coming transition: Fossil capital and our energy future," *Socialism and Democracy,* 30, 2, 2016: 20, 24.

21. Nancy Fraser, *Fortunes of Feminism*, New York: Verso, 2013: 164. Kinder, "The coming transition," 24.

22. Brittany Stares and Kevin Thomas, *Canada's Lobbyist Registries: What Can They Tell Investors about Corporate Lobbying?* Shareholder Association for Research & Education (SHARE), September 2017 <https://share.ca/canadas-lobbyist-registries-need-an-upgrade-report-finds/> accessed 18 September 2017.

23. Jerry Dias and Maude Barlow, "Time for a new narrative on NAFTA." Toronto *Star,* 9 January 2017 <https://www.thestar.com/opinion/commentary/2017/01/09/time-for-a-new-narrative-on-nafta.html> accessed 19 September 2017.

24. "United Nations Declaration on the Rights of Indigenous Peoples" <https://www.un.org/development/desa/indigenouspeoples/declaration-on-the-rights-of-indigenous-peoples.html> accessed 19 September 2017. Rosie Simms, Oliver M. Brandes, Merrell-Ann Phare and Michael Miltenberger, "Collaborative consent is path to govern according to UNDRIP," Vancouver *Sun,* 17 September 2017 <http://vancouversun.com/opinion/op-ed/collaborative-consent-is-path-to-govern-according-to-undrip> accessed 19 September 2017.

25. William K. Carroll and David Huxtable, "Building capacity for alternative knowledge: The Canadian Centre for Policy Alternatives," *Canadian Review of Social Policy,* 70, 2014: 93–111.

26. Guy Aitchison, "How capitalism Is turning the internet against democracy, and how to turn it back," *Znet,* 25 April 2013 <https://zcomm.org/znetarticle/how-capitalism-is-turning-the-internet-against-democracy-and-how-to-turn-

it-back-by-guy-aitchison/> accessed 19 September 2017. Robert A. Hackett and William K. Carroll, *Remaking Media: The Struggle to Democratize Public Communication*, New York: Routledge, 2006: 208.

27. Michelle Williams, "The solidarity economy and social transformation," in Vishwas Satgar (ed.), *The Solidarity Economy Alternative*, Pietermaritzburg, South Africa: University of KwaZulu-Natal Press, 2014: 51. Restakis, *Humanizing the Economy*, 96, 98.

28. Christopher Wright and Daniel Nyberg, *Climate Change, Capitalism, and Corporations*, Cambridge, UK: Cambridge University Press, 2015: 1.

29. Andreas Malm, *Fossil Capital*, London: Verso. Trade Unions for Energy Democracy, 2016 <http://unionsforenergydemocracy.org/> accessed 20 September 2017.

30. Fred Magdoff and John Bellamy Foster, *What Every Environmentalist Needs to Know about Capitalism*, New York: Monthly Review Press, 2011: 120–22. Hartmut Rosa and Christoph Henning (eds.), *The Good Life Beyond Growth: New Perspectives*, London: Routledge, 2018. David Harvey, *Seventeen Contradictions and the End of Capitalism*, New York: Oxford University Press, 2014: 295.

31. Michael A, Lebowitz, *The Socialist Imperative*, New York: Monthly Review Press, 2015: 155. Warren Magnusson, "Private enterprise and public ownership," in Warren Magnusson, Charles Doyle, R.B.J. Walker and John DeMarco (eds.), *After Bennett: A New Politics for British Columbia*, Vancouver: New Star Books, 1986: 95.

REFERENCES

Advisory Council on Economic Growth. 2017. "Unleashing Productivity through Infrastructure." <budget.gc.ca/aceg-ccce/pdf/infrastructure-eng.pdf> accessed August 30, 2017.

Ahmed, Nafeez Mosaddeq. 2017. *Failing States, Collapsing Systems.* Berlin: Springer.

Aitchison, Guy. April 25, 2013. "How capitalism Is turning the internet against democracy, and how to turn it back." *Znet.* <zcomm.org/znetarticle/how-capitalism-is-turning-the-internet-against-democracy-and-how-to-turn-it-back-by-guy-aitchison/> accessed September 19, 2017.

Albo, Gregory. 1993. "Democratic citizenship and the future of public management." In Gregory Albo, David Langille and Leo Panitch (eds.), *A Different Kind of State? Popular Power and Democratic Administration.* Toronto: Oxford University Press.

Albo, Gregory & Fanelli, Carlo. 2014. "Austerity against democracy: An authoritarian phase of neoliberalism?" *Teoria Critica* 4.

Albo, Greg & Yap, Lilian. July 12, 2016. "From the Tar Sands to 'green jobs'? Work and ecological justice." *The Bullet.* <socialistproject.ca/bullet/1280.php> accessed August 16, 2017.

Albritton, Robert. 2007. *Economics Transformed: Discovering the Brilliance of Marx.* London: Pluto Press.

Alook, Angele; Hill, Nicole & Hussey, Ian. June 21, 2017. "Ten things to know about Indigenous people and resource extraction in Alberta." *Corporate Mapping Project.* <www.corporatemapping.ca/ten-things-to-know-about-indigenous-people-and-resource-extraction-in-alberta/> accessed August 16, 2017.

Archives of Manitoba. "Hudson's Bay Company History." <gov.mb.ca/ chc/archives/hbca/about/hbc_history.html> accessed August 1, 2017.

Arthurs, Harry W. 2000. "The hollowing out of corporate Canada?" In Jane Jenson and Boaventura de Sousa Santos (eds.), *Globalizing Institutions: Case Studies in Regulation and Innovation.* Burlington, VT: Ashgate Publishing Company.

Baert, Rick. December 10, 2015. "10 largest Canadian public pension funds' assets top $1 trillion — report." *Pensions and Investments.* <pionline. com/article/20151210/ONLINE/151219992/10-largest-canadian-public-pension-funds-assets-top-1-trillion-8212-report> accessed August 17, 2017.

Bair, Jennifer. 2014. "Editor's introduction: Commodity chains in and of the world system." *Journal of World- Systems Research* 20.

Bakan, Joel. 2004. *The Corporation*, Toronto: Viking Canada.

Barkin, Kenneth D. 1975. "Organized capitalism." *Journal of Modern History* 47, 1.

Barndt, Deborah. 2008. *Tangled Routes*, second edition. Toronto: Rowman & Littlefield.

Blackburn, Robin. December 22, 2005. "A visionary pragmatist." *Counterpunch.* <counterpunch.org/2005/12/22/a-visonary-pragmatist/> accessed September 14, 2017.

Blau, Peter. 1964. *Exchange and Power in Social Life*. New York: John Wiley.

Block, Fred. 1977. "The ruling class does not rule: Notes on the Marxist Theory of the State." *Socialist Revolution* 7, 3.

Boychuk, Regan. 2017. "Ralph Klein's multibillion dollar liability is about to blow up in Alberta's face." *National Observer,* April 3. <nationalobserver.com/2017/04/03/analysis/ralph-kleins-multibillion-dollar-liability-about-blow-albertas-face> accessed July 26, 2017.

Brennan, Jordan. 2012. *A Shrinking Universe: How Concentrated Corporate Capital Is Shaping Income Inequality in Canada*. Ottawa: Canadian Centre for Policy Alternatives, November. <policyalternatives.ca/publications/reports/shrinking-universe> accessed September 5, 2017.

Brownlee, Jamie. 2015. *Academia, Inc: How Corporatization Is Transforming Canadian Universities*. Halifax: Fernwood Publishing.

---. 2005. *Ruling Canada*. Halifax and Winnipeg: Fernwood Publishing.

Bukharin, N.I. 1929. "World Movement of Capital, and Change in the Economic Forms of International Connections" In *Imperialism and World Economy*. New York: International Publishers, Chapter 7. <marxists.org/archive/ bukharin/works/1917/imperial/07.htm> accessed August 6, 2017.

Cakebread, Caroline. 2006. "Global warming." Benefits Canada 30, 4.

Canada. 1937. "Report of the Royal Commission on Price Spreads." Ottawa: King's Printer.

Canadian Association of Petroleum Producers <http://www.energycitizens.ca/>.

Canadian Association of University Teachers. November, 2013. "Open for Business — On What Terms? An Analysis of 12 Collaborations between Canadian Universities and Corporations, Donors and Governments." <caut.ca/docs/default-source/academic-freedom/open-for-business-%28nov-2013%29.pdf?sfvrsn=4> accessed September 2, 2017.

Canadian Business. November 9, 2017. "Canada's Richest People 2018." <canadianbusiness.com/lists-and-rankings/richest-people/top-25-richest-canadians-2018/image/24/> accessed March 2, 2018.

---. December 7, 2017. "Canada's richest people: The complete Top 100 ranking." <canadianbusiness.com/lists-and-rankings/richest-people/100-richest-canadians-complete-list/> accessed March 5, 2018.

Canadian Centre for Policy Alternatives. 2018. "Record-breaking ceo pay now 209 times more than average worker." 2 January 2018 <https://www.policyalternatives.ca/newsroom/news-releases/

record-breaking-ceo-pay-now-209-times-more-average-worker> accessed
March 6, 2018.

---. January 2, 2018. "Record-breaking ceo pay now 209 times more than average
worker." <policyalternatives.ca/newsroom/news-releases/record-breaking-ceo-
pay-now-209-times-more-average-worker> accessed March 6, 2018.

---. n.d. "Alternative Federal Budget." <policyalternatives.ca/projects/ alternative-
federal-budget> accessed September 15, 2017.

Carbon Tracker Initiative and the Grantham Research Institute on Climate Change
and the Environment. n.d. "Unburnable Carbon 2013: Wasted Capital and
Stranded Assets."

Carrington, Damian. 2015. "Fossil fuels subsidized by $10m a minute, says imf." *The
Guardian,* May 18. <theguardian.com/environment/2015/may/18/fossil-fuel-
companies-getting-10m-a-minute-in- subsidies-says-imf> accessed September
2, 2017.

Carroll, William K. 2017. "Canada's carbon-capital elite: A tangled web of corporate
power." *Canadian Journal of Sociology* 42, 3.

---. 2016. "The changing face(s) of corporate power in Canada." In Edward G. Grabb
and Monica Hwang (eds.), *Social Inequality in Canada,* 6th edition, Toronto:
Oxford University Press.

---. 2009. "Corporate interests displace the public interest: Only business leaders
chosen for Economic Advisory Council." *ccpa Monitor* 16, 1, 2009.

---. 2008. "The corporate elite and the transformation of finance capital: A view from
Canada." *Sociological Review* 56, S1.

---. 2007. "From Canadian corporate elite to transnational capitalist class: Transitions
in the organization of corporate power." *Canadian Review of Sociology* 44, 3.

---. 2004. *Corporate Power in a Globalizing World: A Study in Elite Social Organization,*
Don Mills, ON: Oxford University Press.

---. 2003. "Undoing the end of history: Canada-centred reflections on the challenge
of globalization." In Yildiz Atasoy and William K. Carroll (eds.), *Global Shaping
and its Alternatives.* Toronto: Garamond Press.

---. 1986. *Corporate Power and Canadian Capitalism.* Vancouver: ubc Press.

Carroll, William K. & Alexander, Malcolm. 1999. "Finance capital and capitalist class
integration in the 1990s: Networks of interlocking directorships in Canada and
Australia." *Canadian Review of Sociology and Anthropology* 36.

Carroll, William K. & Beaton, James. 2000. "Globalization, Neo-Liberalism, and the
Changing Face of Corporate Hegemony in Higher Education." *Studies in Political
Economy* 62, 1.

Carroll, William K.; Graham, Nicolas; Lang, Michael; McCarthy, Kevin & Yunker, Zoë.
2018. "Carbon capital's reach into civil society: Architecture of climate-change
denialism." *Canadian Review of Sociology* 54, 3.

Carroll, William K.; Graham, Nicolas & Yunker, Zoë. 2018. "Carbon Capital and
Corporate Influence: Mapping Elite Networks of Corporations, Universities
and Research Institutes." In Jamie Brownlee, Christopher Hurl and Kevin Walby
(eds.), *Corporatizing Canada: Making Business out of Public Service.* Toronto:
Between the Lines.

Carroll, William K. & Huxtable, David. 2014. "Building capacity for alternative knowledge: The Canadian Centre for Policy Alternatives." *Canadian Review of Social Policy* 70.

Carroll, William K. & Klassen, Jerome. 2010. "Hollowing out corporate Canada? Changes in the Corporate Network since the 1990s." *Canadian Journal of Sociology* 35.

Carroll William K. & Lewis, Scott. 1991. "Restructuring finance capital: Changes in the Canadian corporate network 1976–1986." *Sociology* 25.

Carroll William K. & Shaw, Murray. 2001. "Consolidating a neoliberal policy bloc in Canada, 1976–1996." *Canadian Public Policy* 27, 2.

Carter, Angela V. & Zalik, Anna. 2016. "Fossil capitalism and the rentier state: Toward a political ecology of Alberta's oil economy," in Laurie E. Adkin (ed.), *First World Petro-Politics: The Political Ecology and Governance of Alberta*. Toronto: University of Toronto Press.

CBC News. January 29, 2018. "Nearly 100 homeless people died in Toronto in 2017." <cbc.ca/news/canada/toronto/homeless-deaths-toronto-public-health-1.4509218> accessed March 6, 2018.

---. January 24, 2017. "A chronological history of controversial Keystone XL pipeline project." <http://www.cbc.ca/news/politics/keystone-xl-pipeline-timeline-1.3950156> accessed September 12, 2017.

CD Howe Institute. 2017. "Lifting Living Standards One Donation at a Time: Report on Giving 2017." Toronto.

Chan, Jenny; Lizhi, Xu & Yang. 2015. *Lamachine est ton seigneur et ton maître*. Marseille: Agone.

Clement, Wallace. 1977. *Continental Corporate Power*, Toronto: McClelland & Stewart.

---. 1975. *The Canadian Corporate Elite*. Toronto: McClelland & Stewart.

Coburn, Elaine & Atleo, Cliff (Kam'ayaam/Chachim'multhnii). 2016. "Not just another social movement: Indigenous resistance and resurgence." In William K. Carroll and Kanchan Sarker (eds.), *A World to Win: Contemporary Social Movements and Counter-Hegemony*. Winnipeg: ARP Books.

Cole, Trevor. 1998. "Ivy-League Hustle." *Report on Business Magazine* 14, 12.

Coulthard, Glen Sean. 2014. *Red Skin, White Masks*. Minneapolis: University of Minnesota Press.

CPP Investment Board. n.d. Canadian Publicly-Traded Equity Holdings. <cppib.com/documents/1604/cdn_publicequityholdings_Mar2017_en.htm> accessed August 17, 2017.

---. n.d. Foreign Publicly-Traded Equity Holdings. <cppib.com/documents/1606/foreign_publicequityholdings_Mar2017_en.htm> accessed August 17, 2017.

Craven, Paul, & Traves, Tom. 1979. "The class politics of the National Policy, 1872–1933." *Journal of Canadian Studies*.

Cross, Philip & Bergevin, Philippe. 2012. *Turning Points: Business Cycles in Canada since 1926*. Toronto: CD Howe Institute, Commentary No. 355.

Daub, Shannon & Carroll, Bill. 2016. "Why is the ceo of a big Canadian bank giving speeches about climate change and pipelines?" *Corporate Mapping Project*, October 6. <corporatemapping.ca/rbc-ceo-speech-climate- pipelines/> accessed

August 21, 2017.

Dean, Jodi. 2013. *The Communist Horizon*. London: Verso.

De Grass, Richard P. 1977. "Development of monopolies in Canada from 1907–1913." Master's thesis, University of Waterloo.

Department of Finance. March 18, 2016. "Minister Morneau announces membership of the Advisory Council on Economic Growth." Ottawa. <fin.gc.ca/n16/16-031-eng.asp> accessed August 30, 2017.

DeSmog Canada. July 2, 2014 <www.desmog.org> reprinted with permission of Alex McLean.

Dias, Jerry & Barlow, Maude. January 9, 2017. "Time for a new narrative on nafta." *Toronto Star*. <thestar.com/opinion/commentary/2017/01/09/ time-for-a-new-narrative-on-nafta.html> accessed September 19, 2017.

Dobbin, Murray. 1998. *The Myth of the Good Corporate Citizen: Democracy Under the Rule of Big Business*. Toronto: Stoddart.

Domhoff, G. William. 2006. *Who Rules America?* New York: McGraw-Hill.

Drache, Daniel. 1970. "The Canadian bourgeoisie and its national consciousness." In Ian Lumsden (ed.), *Close the 49th Parallel etc: The Americanization of Canada*. Toronto: University of Toronto Press.

Edwards, Richard. 1979. *Contested Terrain*. New York: Basic Books.

Elliott, Larry. April 8, 2015. "Can the world economy survive without fossil fuels?" *The Guardian*. <theguardian.com/news/2015/apr/08/can-world-economy-survive-without-fossil-fuels> accessed October 26, 2017.

Engelhardt, Tom. February 23, 2009. "As GM goes, so goes…" *The Nation*. <thenation.com/article/gm-goes-so-goes/> accessed February 22, 2018.

Erçel, Kenan. 2006. "Orientalization of exploitation: A class-analytical critique of the sweatshop discourse." *Rethinking Marxism* 18, 2.

Fine, Ben. 1984. *Marx's Capital*. London: Macmillan.

Fleming, R.B. 2007. *The Railway King of Canada: Sir William Mackenzie, 1849–1923*. Vancouver: ubc Press.

Fox, John & Ornstein, Michael D. 1986. "The Canadian State and Corporate Elites in the Post-War Period." *Canadian Review of Sociology and Anthropology* 23, 1986.

Fraser Institute. 2016. Annual Report. Vancouver.

Fraser, Nancy. 2013. *Fortunes of Feminism*. New York: Verso.

Fuchs, Christian. 2012. "Dallas Smythe today — the audience commodity, the digital labour debate, Marxist political economy and critical theory. Prolegomena to a digital labour theory of value." *tripleC* 10, 2.

Gadhoum, Yoser. 2006. "Power of ultimate controlling owners: A survey of Canadian landscape." *Journal of Management Governance* 10.

Gamble, Andrew. 1988. *The Free Economy and the Strong State*. New York: Macmillan.

GBL. n.d. "GBL Management" <gbl.be/en/team> accessed August 18, 2017.

Gereffi, Gary & Korzeniewicz, Miguel. 1994. *Commodity Chains and Global Capitalism*. Westport, CT: Greenwood Press/Praeger.

Gill, Stephen & Law, David. 2003. "The power of capital: Direct and structural." In Stephen Gill, *Power and Resistance in the New World Order*. New York: Palgrave Macmillan.

Government of Canada. 2018. "A Modern, New and World-Class Federal Energy Regulator for the 21st Century."

---. n.d. <international.gc.ca/csr_counsellor- conseiller_rse/index.aspx?lang=eng> accessed August 31, 2017.

Graham, Nicolas; Daub, Shannon & Carroll, Bill. 2017. *Mapping Political Influence: Political Donations and Lobbying by the Fossil Fuel Industry in BC.* Vancouver: Canadian Centre for Policy Alternatives.

Gramsci, Antonio. 1971. "The intellectuals." In *Selections from the Prison Notebooks,* New York: International Publishers.

---. 1971. *Selections from the Prison Notebooks.* London: Lawrence and Wishart.

Granger, Alix. 2017. "Banking in Canada." *Canadian Encyclopedia.* <thecanadianencyclopedia.ca/en/article/banking/> accessed September 5, 2017.

Green, Joyce A. 2003. "Decolonization and recolonization in Canada." In Wallace Clement and Leah Vosco (eds.), *Changing Canada: Political Economy as Transformation.* Montreal: McGill-Queen's University Press.

---. 1995. "Towards a détente with history: Confronting Canada's colonial legacy." *International Journal of Canadian Studies* 12 (Fall).

Griffin, Paul. 2017. *cdp Carbon Majors Report 2017,* London: cdp. <cdp.net/en/reports/archive> accessed August 9, 2017.

Gunster, Shane & Saurette, Paul. 2014. "Storylines in the sands: News, narrative and ideology in the Calgary Herald." *Canadian Journal of Communication* 39, 3.

Gutstein, Donald. 2014. *Harperism: How Stephen Harper and his think tanks colleagues have transformed Canada."* Toronto: Lorimer.

Hackett, Robert A. & Carroll, William K. 2006. *Remaking Media: The Struggle to Democratize Public Communication.* New York: Routledge.

Harnecker, Marta. 2015. *A World to Build.* New York: Monthly Review Press.

Harvey, David. 2014. *Seventeen Contradictions and the End of Capitalism.* New York: Oxford University Press.

Heede, Richard. 2014. "Tracing anthropogenic carbon dioxide and methane emissions to fossil fuel and cement producers, 1854–2010". *Climate Change,* 122.

Henwood, Doug. 1992. "Financial crisis averted?" *Left Business Observer* 56, December. <leftbusinessobserver.com/Financial-crisis-averted.html> accessed August 22, 2017.

Hilary, John. 2013. *The Poverty of Capitalism.* London: Pluto Press.

Hilferding, Rudolf. 1981 [1910]. *Finance Capital: A Study of the Latest Phase of Capitalist Development.* London: Routledge & K. Paul.

Hill, Gord. 2009. *500 Years of Indigenous Resistance.* Oakland, CA: PM Press.

Hoare, Quintin & Nowell Smith, Geoffrey. 1971. "State and civil society." In Quintin Hoare and Geoffrey Nowell Smith (eds.), *Selections from the Prison Notebooks of Antonio Gramsci,* International Publishers.

Holmes, John. 1988. "Industrial restructuring in a period of crisis: An analysis of the Canadian automobile industry, 1973–83." *Antipode* 20, 1.

Horne, Gerald. 2014. *The Counter-Revolution of 1776.* New York: New York University Press.

Huber, Matthew T. 2013. *Lifeblood: Oil, Freedom, and the Forces of Capital.*

Minneapolis: University of Minnesota Press.

Hughes, David. 2016. "Can Canada expand oil and gas production, build pipelines and keep its climate change commitments?" Vancouver: Canadian Centre for Policy Alternatives. <policyalternatives.ca/more-than-enough> accessed September 13, 2017.

Hussein, Athar. 1976. "Hilferding's finance capital." *Bulletin of the Conference of Socialist Economists* 5, 1.

Insurance Hunter.ca. October 20, 2017. "Even though Sears Canada is closing, execs will receive bonuses." <insurancehunter.ca/news/even-though-sears-canada-closing-execs-will-receive-bonuses> accessed October 26, 2017.

Irving, J.D. n.d. "History." <jdirving.com/jd-irving-about-us-history.aspx> accessed March 12, 2018.

Jessop, Bob. 2016. *The State: Past, Present, Future*, Cambridge: Polity Press.

Johnson, Leo A. 1977. *Poverty in Wealth: The Capitalist Labour Market and Income Distribution in Canada*. Toronto: New Hogtown Press.

Kamlani, Tarannum. 2013. "Made in Bangladesh." *The Fifth Estate, cbc Radio-Canada*. <cbc.ca/fifth/episodes/2013-2014/made-in-bangladesh> accessed August 15, 2017.

Kanji, Azeezah. 2018. "Imagine cities that shelter people, not war," *Toronto Star*, January 11. <www.thestar.com/opinion/contributors/2018/01/11/ imagine-cities-that-shelter-people-not-war.html> accessed 6 March, 2018.

Kellogg, Paul. 2015. *Escape from the Staples Trap*. Toronto: University of Toronto Press.

Kinder, Jordan. 2016. "The coming transition: Fossil capital and our energy future." *Socialism and Democracy* 30, 2.

Klassen, Jerome. 2014. *Joining Empire*. Toronto: University of Toronto Press.

Klassen, Jerome & Carroll, William K. 2011. "Transnational Class Formation? Globalization and the Canadian Corporate Network." *Journal of World-Systems Research* 17.

Kogut, Bruce (ed.). 2012. *The Small Worlds of Corporate Governance*. Boston: MIT Press.

Kopun, Francin. January 31, 2018. "Loblaw, Walmart, Sobeys, Metro, Giant Tiger allegedly involved in alleged bread price-fixing scheme: Court documents." *Toronto Star*. <thestar.com/business/2018/01/31/ at-least-7-companies-committed-indictable-offences-in-bread-price-fixing- scandal-competition-bureau.html> accessed March 2, 2018.

---. October 26, 2017. "Sears Canada pensioners demand shortfall be paid off first." *Toronto Star*. <thestar.com/business/2017/10/26/ sears-canada-pensioners-demand-shortfall-be-paid-off-first.html> accessed October 26, 2017.

Kwak, James. 2014. "Cultural capture and the financial crisis." In Daniel Carpenter and David Moss (eds.), Preventing Regulatory Capture: Special Interest Influence and How to Limit It. Cambridge University Press. <tobinproject.org/sites/ tobinproject.org/files/assets/Kwak%20-%20Cultural%20Capture%20and%20 the%20Financial%20Crisis.pdf> accessed August 30, 2017.

LafargeHolcim. n.d. LafargeHolcim board of directors. <lafargeholcim.com/board-directors> accessed August 18, 2017.

Langille, David. 1987. "The Business Council on National Issues and the Canadian state." *Studies in Political Economy* 24.

Lash, Scott & Urry, John. 1987. *The End of Organized Capitalism*. Madison, WI: University of Wisconsin Press.

Laxer, Gordon. 2015. *After the Sands*. Madeira Park, BC: Douglas & McIntyre.

Leahy, Stephen. October 1, 2014. "Canada is now the world's leading 'deforestation nation." *Rabble*. <rabble.ca/columnists/2014/10/canada-now-worlds-leading-deforestation-nation> accessed August 3, 2017.

Lebowitz, Michael A. 2015. *The Socialist Imperative*. New York: Monthly Review Press.

---. 1992. *Beyond Capital*. London: Macmillan.

Levitt, Kari. 1970. *Silent Surrender*. Toronto: Macmillan of Canada.

Linnittemists, Carole. February 17, 2015. "'Threat to government and industry." *DeSmogCanada*. "LEAKED: Internal RCMP document names 'violent anti-petroleum extremists'" <desmog.ca/2015/02/17/leaked-internal-rcmp-document-names-anti-petroleum- extremists-threat-government-industry> accessed September 2, 2017.

Livesey, Bruce. May 5, 2017. "Spies in our midst: RCMP and CSIS snoop on green activists." *National Observer*. <nationalobserver.com/2017/05/05/news/spies-our-midst-rcmp-and-csis-snoop- green-activists> accessed September 2, 2017.

---. June 16, 2016. "What have the Irvings done to New Brunswick?" *National Observer*. <nationalobserver.com/2016/06/06/news/ what-have-irvings-done-new-brunswick> accessed March 12, 2018.

Lowe, Graham S. 1982. "Class, job and gender in the Canadian office." *Labour/Le Travail* 10.

Lukawiecki, Jessica & Gosset, Laura. January 9, 2017. "Taking climate on board: Are Canadian energy and utilities company boards equipped to address climate change?" Vancouver: Shareholder Association for Research & Education. <share.ca/publications/issue-briefs/> accessed September 14, 2017.

Macdonald, David. 2014. *Outrageous Fortune: Documenting Canada's Wealth Gap*. Ottawa: Canadian Centre for Policy Alternatives.

---. April 30, 2012. *The Big Banks' Big Secret: Estimating Government Support for Canadian Banks During the Financial Crisis*. Ottawa: Canadian Centre for Policy Alternatives. <policyalternatives.ca/publications/reports/big-banks-big-secret> accessed September 15, 2017.

Mackenzie, Hugh. January 3, 2017. *Throwing Money at the Problem: 10 years of Executive Compensation in Canada*. Ottawa: Canadian Centre for Policy Alternatives. <policyalternatives.ca/ceo2017> accessed August 17, 2017.

Magdoff, Fred & Foster, John Bellamy. 2011. *What Every Environmentalist Needs to Know about Capitalism*. New York: Monthly Review Press.

Magnusson, Warren. 1986. "Private enterprise and public ownership." In Warren Magnusson, Charles Doyle, R.B.J. Walker and John DeMarco (eds.), *After Bennett: A New Politics for British Columbia*. Vancouver: New Star Books.

Mahon, Rianne. 1984. *The Politics of Industrial Restructuring*. Toronto: University of Toronto Press 41, 39.

Malleson, Tom. 2016. *Fired up about Capitalism*. Toronto: Between the Lines.

Malm, Andreas. 2016. *Fossil Capital.* London: Verso.

Mandel, Ernest. 1968. *Marxist Economic Theory.* London: Merlin Press.

Marglin, S.A. 1974. "What do bosses do? The origins and functions of hierarchy in Capitalist production." *Review of Radical Political Economics* 6, 2.

Markusoff, Jason. January 11, 2018. "Loblaw's price-fixing may have cost you at least $400." *Maclean's.* <macleans.ca/economy/economicanalysis/14-years-of-loblaws-bread-price-fixing-may-have-cost-you-at-least-400/> accessed March 2, 2018.

Marx, Karl. 2004 [1845]. "Theses on Feurbach." In William K. Carroll (ed.), *Critical Strategies for Social Research.* Toronto: Canadian Scholar's Press.

---. 1999 [1847]. *The Poverty of Philosophy.* Marx/Engels Internet Archive, Chapter 2 <marxists.org/archive/marx/works/1847/poverty-philosophy/ch02e.htm> accessed August 11, 2017.

---. 1996 [1894]. *Capital, Vol. 3.* New York: International Publishers: Chapter 27. <marxists.org/archive/marx/works/1894-c3/ch27.htm> accessed August 3, 2017.

---. 1887 [1867]. *Capital: A Critique of Political Economy, Vol. 1,* translated by Samuel Moore and Edward Aveling. <https://www.marxists.org/archive/ marx/works/1867-c1/ch33.htm> accessed July 24, 2017.

---. 1857. "Capital as Fructiferous: Transformation of Surplus Value into Profit." *Grundrisse.* <marxists.org/archive/marx/works/1857/ grundrisse/ch15.htm> accessed July 25, 2017.

---. n.d. "Fictitious Capital." *Marxist Internet Archive.* <https://www.marxists.org/ glossary/terms/f/i.htm> accessed August 22, 2017.

Marx, Karl & Engels, Frederick. 2000 [1848]. "Bourgeois and proletarians." In *Manifesto of the Communist Party,* Marx/Engels Internet Archive, Chapter I <marxists.org/archive/marx/works/1848/communist-manifesto/ch01.htm#007> accessed August 14, 2017.

McCarthy, Shawn. May 15, 2017. "National Energy Board needs major overhaul, panel says," Toronto: *Globe and Mail.* <theglobeandmail.com/report-on-business/ industry-news/energy-and-resources/dismantle-neb-create-bodies-for-regulation-growth-panel/article34989230/?ref=http://www.theglobeandmail. com&> accessed September 12, 2017.

McClelland, J.L. 1929. "The merger movement in Canada since 1880." Master's thesis, Queen's University.

McCormack, Geoffrey & Workman, Thom. 2015. *The Servant State.* Winnipeg and Halifax: Fernwood.

McKay, Ian. 2005. *Rebels, Reds, Radicals: Rethinking Canada's Left History.* Toronto: Between the Lines.

McNally, David. 2006. *Another World Is Possible,* second edition. Winnipeg: Arbeiter Ring Publishing.

Meidner, Rudolf. 1993. "Why did the Swedish model fail?" In Ralph Miliband and Leo Panitch (eds), *Socialist Register 1993,* London: Merlin Press.

Meiksins Wood, Ellen. 1981. "The separation of the economic and the political in capitalism." *New Left Review* 127.

Miliband, Ralph. 1983. "State power and class interests." *New Left Review* 138.

Minsky, Amy. June 15, 2017. "Average hourly wages in Canada have barely budged in 40 years." *Global News.* <globalnews.ca/news/3531614/average-hourly-wage-canada-stagnant/> accessed September 12, 2017.

Mintz, Beth & Schwartz, Michael. 1985. *The Power Structure of American Business.* Chicago: University of Chicago Press.

Model, David. 2003. *Corporate Rule.* Montreal: Black Rose Books.

Moore, Jason W. 2015. *Capitalism in the Web of Life: Ecology and the Accumulation of Capital.* London: Verso.

Milner, Henry & Hodgins Milner, Sheilagh. 1973. *The Decolonization of Quebec.* Toronto: McClelland & Stewart.

Mitchell, Timothy. 2011. *Carbon Democracy.* London: Verso.

Mosca, Gaetano. 1939. *The Ruling Class.* McGraw-Hill.

Myers, Gustavus. 1975 [1914]. *A History of Canadian Wealth.* Toronto: James Lorimer.

National Energy Board. 2017. "Estimated production of Canadian crude oil and equivalent." <neb-one.gc.ca/nrg/sttstc/crdlndptrlmprdct/stt/stmtdprdctn-eng.html> accessed October 29, 2017.

Naylor R.T. 1972. "The rise and fall of the third commercial empire of the St Lawrence." In Gary Teeple (ed.), *Capitalism and the National Question in Canada.* Toronto: University of Toronto Press.

Nesbit, Jeff. 2016. *Poison Tea: How Big Oil and Big Tobacco Invested the Tea Party and Captured the gop.* New York: St. Martin's Press. <energycitizens.ca/> accessed August 31, 2017.

Newman, Peter C. 1998. *Titans: How the New Canadian Establishment Seized Power.* Toronto: Viking.

Nikiforuk, Andrew. June 28, 2017. "Energy industry legacy: Hundreds of abandoned wells leaking methane in Alberta communities," *The Tyee.* <thetyee.ca/News/2017/06/28/Energy-Industry-Legacy/?utm_source=daily&utm_medium=email&utm_campaign=280617> accessed July 26, 2017.

---. February 9, 2017. "On oil spills, Alberta regulator can't be believed: New report." *The Tyee.* <thetyee.ca/News/2017/02/09/Oil- Spills-Alberta-Regulator/> accessed August 30, 2017.

Niosi, Jorge. 1985. *Canadian Multinationals.* Toronto: Between the Lines.

---. 1981. *Canadian Capitalism.* Toronto: Lorimer.

---. 1978. *The Economy of Canada: Who Controls It?* Montreal: Black Rose Books.

Nock, David A. 1976. "The intimate connection: Links between the political and economic systems in Canadian federal politics." Doctoral dissertation, University of Alberta.

Nuttall, Jeremy. July 14, 2017. "Mount Polley disaster brought quick government PR response, documents show." *The Tyee.* <thetyee.ca/ News/2017/07/14/Mount-Polley-Disaster-Government-PR-Response/> accessed July 26, 2017.

O'Connor, James. 1998. *Natural Causes,* New York: Guilford Press.

---. 1973. *The Fiscal Crisis of the State,* New York: St. Martin's Press.

Office of the Senate Ethics Officer. 2014. "Conflict of Interest Code for Senators." Senate of Canada. <sen. parl.gc.ca/seo-cse/PDF/Code-e.pdf> accessed August 30, 2017.

Olin Wright, Erik. 1985. *Classes.* London: Verso,

Ornstein, Michael D. 1989. "The social organization of the Canadian capitalist class in comparative perspective." *Canadian Review of Sociology and Anthropology* 26.

Overbeek, Henk. 1980. "Finance capital and the crisis in Britain." *Capital & Class,* 2.

Panitch, Leo. December 4, 2008. "From the global crisis to Canada's crisis." Toronto: Globe and Mail. <beta.theglobeandmail.com/ opinion/from-the-global-crisis-to-canadas-crisis/article22502333/?ref=http:// www.theglobeandmail.com&> accessed September 16, 2017.

Panitch, Leo. 1977. "The development of corporatism in liberal democracies." *Comparative Political Studies* 10, 1.

Palley, Thomas I. June 2000. "Destabilizing speculation and the case for an international currency transactions tax." *Global Policy Forum.* <globalpolicy.org/social-and-economic-policy/global-taxes-1-79/currency-transaction-taxes/45990-destabilizing-speculation-and-the-case-for-an-international-currency-transactions-tax.html> accessed September 15, 2017.

Park, Libbie & Park, Frank. 1962. *Anatomy of Big Business,* Toronto: Progress Books.

Participatory Economics: A Model for a New Economy. n.d. "Balanced jobs." <participatoryeconomics.info/institutions/balanced-jobs/> accessed September 14, 2017.

Parkin, Frank. 1979. *Marxism and Class Theory: A Bourgeois Critique.* London: Tavistock Publications.

Pentland, H. Claire. 1981. *Labour and Capital in Canada 1650–1860.* Toronto: James Lorimer.

Perlo, Victor. 1958. "'People's Capitalism' and stock ownership." *American Economic Review* 48.

Pineault, Éric. 2018. "The capitalist pressure to extract, an ecological and political economy of extreme oil in Canada." *Studies in Political Economy* 99.

Piédalue, Gilles. 1976. "Les groupes financiers au Canada 1900–1930." *Revue d'histoire de l'Amérique française* 30, 1.

Pollin, Robert; Baker, Dean & Schaberg, Marc. 2002. *Securities Transaction Taxes for US Financial Markets.* PERI Working Paper No. 20. <papers.ssrn.com/sol3/papers.cfm?abstract_id=333742> accessed September 15, 2017.

Porter, John. 1965. *The Vertical Mosaic.* Toronto: University of Toronto Press.

Power Corporation. n.d. Power Corporation of Canada organization chart. <powercorporation.com/en/companies/organization-chart/> accessed August 18, 2017.

---. n.d. Power Corporation of Canada financial highlights. <powercorporation. com/en/investors/financial-highlights/> accessed August 18, 2017.

Public Safety Canada. 2017. National Strategy for Critical Infrastructure. <publicsafety.gc.ca/cnt/rsrcs/pblctns/srtg-crtcl-nfrstrctr/index-en.aspx> accessed August 22, 2017.

---. 2014. Action Plan for Critical Infrastructure (2014–2017). <publicsafety.gc.ca/cnt/rsrcs/pblctns/pln-crtcl-nfrstrctr-2014-17/index-en.aspx> accessed September 2, 2017.

Pupo, Norene & Thomas, Mark. 2009. "Work in the new economy: Critical reflections." In Noreen Pupo and Mark Thomas (eds.), *Interrogating the New Economy:*

Restructuring Work in the 21st Century. Toronto: University of Toronto Press, 2009.

Raso, Kathleen & Neubauer, Robert Joseph. 2016. "Managing dissent: Energy pipelines and 'new right' politics in Canada." *Canadian Journal of Communication* 41, 1.

The Regina Manifesto (1933) Co-operative Commonwealth Federation Programme <socialisthistory.ca/Docs/CCF/ReginaManifesto.htm> accessed September 15, 2017.

Rees, William E. 2014. "Avoiding collapse: An agenda for sustainable degrowth and relocalizing the economy." Vancouver: Canadian Centre for Policy Alternatives, BC Office.

Reford, Alexander. 1998. "Smith, Donald Alexander, 1st Baron Strathcona and Mount Royal." In *Dictionary of Canadian Biography*, vol. 14, University of Toronto/ Université Laval. <biographi.ca/en/bio/smith_donald_ alexander_14E.html> accessed August 2, 2017.

Restakis, John. 2010. *Humanizing the Economy: Co-operatives in the Age of Capital.* Gabriola Island, BC: New Society Publishers.

Rinehart, James W. 1975. *The Tyranny of Work.* Toronto: Longman.

Robinson, William I. 2004. *A Theory of Global Capitalism,* Baltimore: Johns Hopkins University Press, 2004.

Rogers, Chris. 2014. *Capitalism and its Alternatives.* London: Zed Books.

Rosa, Hartmut & Henning, Christoph (eds.). 2018. The Good Life Beyond *Growth: New Perspectives.* London: Routledge.

Rowe, James; Peredo, Ana Maria & Restakis, John. July 27, 2017. "How the ndp and Greens can grow BC's cooperative economy." *The Tyee.* <thetyee. ca/ Opinion/2017/07/27/BC-NDP-Greens-Can-Grow-Co-op-Economy/?utm_ source=daily&utm_medium=email&utm_campaign=270717> accessed September 14, 2017.

Rowley, Elizabeth. June 29, 2017. "Bill C-59: Another threat to democracy." *People's Voice.*<peoplesvoice.ca/2017/06/29/bill-c-59-another-threat-to-democracy/> accessed September 2, 2017.

Saad-Filho, Alfredo. 2003. "Value, capital and exploitation." in Alfredo Saad-Filho (ed.), *Anti-Capitalism,* London: Pluto Press.

Schnaiberg, Allan. 1980. *The Environment: From Surplus to Scarcity.* New York: Oxford University Press.

Scott, John. 1997. *Corporate Business and Capitalist Classes.* New York: Oxford University Press.

Sears, Alan. 2003. *Retooling the Mind Factory.* Aurora, ON: Garamond Press.

Sefton MacDowell, Laurel. 2012. *An Environmental History of Canada.* Vancouver: ubc Press.

Shaw, Holly. February 14, 2018. "Sears retirees seek trustee to help recoup part of $3 billion in dividends paid to shareholders." *Financial Post.* <business.financialpost. com/news/retail-marketing/sears-retirees-seek-appointment-of-trustee-to-help-recoup-part-of-the-3b-in-dividends-paid-to-shareholders> accessed March 7, 2018.

Simms, Rosie; Brandes, Oliver M.; Phare Merrell-Ann & Michael Miltenberger. September 17, 2017. "Collaborative consent is path to govern according to undrip"

Vancouver Sun. <vancouversun.com/opinion/op-ed/collaborative-consent-is-path-to-govern- according-to-undrip> accessed September 19, 2017.

Smith, Dorothy E. 1985. "Women, class and family." In Roxana Ng (ed.), *Women, Class, Family and the State.* Toronto: Garamond Press.

Smythe, Dallas. 1994. *Counterclockwise.* Boulder, CO: Westview Press.

SNC-Lavalin. 2016. "Annual Report 2015." Montréal: snc-Lavalin.

Sorenson, Chris. September 29, 2014. "The interview: Jacques Poitras on the Irving family dynasty." *Maclean's.* <macleans.ca/economy/business/the-interview-jacques-poitras-on-the-irving-family-dynasty/> accessed March 12, 2018.

Stares, Brittany & Thomas, Kevin. September 2017. *Canada's Lobbyist Registries: What Can They Tell Investors about Corporate Lobbying?* Shareholder Association for Research & Education (SHARE). <share.ca/canadas-lobbyist- registries-need-an-upgrade-report-finds/> accessed September 18, 2017.

Starr, Douglas. August 25, 2016. "Just 90 companies are to blame for most climate change, this 'carbon accountant' says." *Science.* <sciencemag. org/news/2016/08/just-90-companies-are-blame-most-climate-change-carbon- accountant-says> accessed July 27, 2017.

Statistics Canada. 2017. Gross domestic product, expenditure-based. <statcan.gc.ca/tables-tableaux/sum-som/l01/cst01/econ04-eng.htm> accessed August 21, 2017.

---. n.d. Table 380-0076, Current and capital accounts – Corporations, annual (accessed September 17, 2017).

Statistics Canada Daily. September 8, 2017. "Labour Force Survey, August 2017." <statcan.gc.ca/daily-quotidien/170908/dq170908a-eng.htm> accessed September 12, 2017.

Stendie, Larissa & Adkin, Laurie E. 2016. "In the path of the pipeline: Environmental citizenship, Aboriginal rights, and the Northern Gateway Pipeline Review." In Laurie E. Adkin (ed.), *First World Petro-Politics: The Political Ecology and Governance of Alberta.* Toronto: University of Toronto Press.

Stoymenoff, Alexis. April 25, 2012. "'Charitable' Fraser Institute accepted $500K in foreign funding from Koch oil billionnaires." *Vancouver Observer.* <vancouverobserver.com/politics/2012/04/25/charitable-fraser-institute-accepted-500k-foreign-funding-oil-billionaires> accessed February 2, 2018.

Swift, Richard. 2014. S.O.S. Alternatives to Capitalism. Toronto: Between the Lines.

Tobin, James. April 1, 2011. "The case for a tax on international monetary transactions." Canadian Centre for Policy Alternatives Monitor. <policyalternatives.ca/publications/monitor/tobin-tax> accessed September 15, 2017.

Tough, Frank J. 1992. "Aboriginal rights versus the deed of surrender: The legal rights of Native peoples and Canada's Acquisition of the Hudson's Bay Company Territory." *Prairie Forum* 17, 2. <iportal.usask.ca/index.php?cat=276&t=subpages> accessed August 1, 2017.

Trade Unions for Energy Democracy. 2016 <http://unionsforenergydemocracy.org/> accessed September 20, 2017.

TransCanada. 2017. "We've accomplished a lot in seven decades." 2017. <https://www.transcanada. com/en/about/our-history/> accessed August 19, 2017.

Transnational Institute. February 1, 2006. "Participatory budgeting in Canada." <tni.

org/es/node/13963#10> accessed September 15, 2017.

"United Nations Declaration on the Rights of Indigenous Peoples" <un.org/development/desa/indigenouspeoples/declaration-on-the-rights-of- indigenous-peoples.html> accessed September 19, 2017.

Urry, John. 1981. *Anatomy of Capitalist Societies*. London: Macmillan.

Useem, Michael. 1984. *The Inner Circle*. New York: Oxford University Press.

Veldhuis, Niels. 2017. "Fraser Institute ranked top think-tank in Canada, 11th best independent think-tank worldwide." Fraser Institute. <fraserinstitute.org/studies/fraser-institute-ranked-top-think-tank-in-canada-11th-best-independent-think-tank-worldwide> accessed August 29, 2017.

VeneKlasen, Lisa & Miller, Valerie. 2007. *A New Weave of Power, People, and Politics: The Action for Advocacy and Citizen Participation*, Warwickshire, U.K.: Practical Action Pub.

Williams, Michelle. 2014. "The solidarity economy and social transformation." In Vishwas Satgar (ed.), *The Solidarity Economy Alternative*. Pietermaritzburg, South Africa: University of KwaZulu-Natal Press.

Wilt, James. March 23, 2017. "Alberta's pipeline regulation a 'facade': experts." *Desmog Canada*. <desmog.ca/2017/03/23/alberta-s-pipeline-regulation-facade-experts?utm_source=Newsletter&utm_medium=DSCWeekly&utm_campaign=March_30_2017> accessed August 30, 2017.

Winseck, Dwayne. November 22, 2016. "Poster: Mapping Canada's top telecoms, internet & media companies by revenue and market share (2015)." Canadian Media Concentration Research Project. <cmcrp.org/poster-mapping-canadas-top-telecoms- internet-media-companies-by-revenue-and-market-share-2015/> accessed September 12, 2017.

World Bank. September 11, 2017. "5-Bank Asset Concentration for Canada [DDO106CAA156NWDB]." Retrieved from FRED, Federal Reserve Bank of St. Louis <fred.stlouisfed.org/series/DDO106CAA156NWDB>.

Wolfe, David A. 1984. "The rise and demise of the Keynesian era in Canada: Economic policy, 1930–1982." In Michael S. Cross and Gregory S. Kealey (eds.), *Modern Canada 1930s–1980s*. Toronto: McClelland & Stewart.

Wood, Roderick J. 2013. "Corporation Law." *The Canadian Encyclopedia*. <thecanadianencyclopedia.ca/en/article/corporation-law/> accessed August 4, 2017.

Wright, Christopher & Nyberg, Daniel. 2015. *Climate Change, Capitalism, and Corporations*. Cambridge, UK: Cambridge University Press.

INDEX